PRAYERS OF THE SOUL
Prayers for different circumstances in life

PRAYERS OF THE SOUL

Prayers for different circumstances in life

English version of the Spanish original
with extra beautiful Prayers to St Joseph

Fr. Juan Carlos Gavancho

Title of the Spanish original
Plegarias del Alma

Translated by Fr. Juan Carlos Gavancho in cooperation
with
Fr. Charles Fanelli
Ms. Margaret Boharic
Mr. Martin Nyberg
Mrs. Alice Drennan
Ms. Jessica Therriault
Mrs. Christine von Mallinckrodf
Mrs. Liz Overholt
Mr. Wayne and Mrs. Miriam Smith

Cover by
Ms. Alejandra Chavarry

© First English edition: July 2021
All rights reserved.
ISBN: 9798520764564
Library of Congress Control Number: 2021913742
Printed in the United States of América.

I would like to dedicate this book to my mother, Rosa Hurtado de Gavancho who in her bosom taught me to pray and put God always first; and to my Baptism godmother, Irma Peralta Virú, example of kindness and gentleness.

Table of Contents

1. Prayer Life and Grace 13
2. Who does God listen to? 14
   - 2.1. Dependence on God and spiritual poverty 15
   - 2.2. Humility and sincere recognition of our misery 20
3. Prayer and suffering 26
4. "Lord, teach us how to pray" (Lc 11: 1) 30
5. Faith and Vocal Prayer 32
6. "Prayers of the soul" 36

I DAILY PRAYERS AND DEVOTIONS DIRECTED TO GOD 41

1. Morning prayer 43
1. Night prayer I 44
2. Night Prayer II 45
3. Act of contrition 45
4. Prayer before the Holy Mass I 46
5. Prayer before Holy Mass II 48
6. Prayer after the Holy Mass I 49
7. Prayer after the Holy Mass II 49
8. Prayer after sacramental confession 50
9. Prayer of consecration to the Heart of Jesus 51
10. Prayer of the priest before Holy Mass. 52
11. Prayer of the priest after the Holy Mass 54
12. Act of reparation 55
13. Prayer of abandonment 56
14. Beginning mental prayer I 57
15. Beginning mental prayer II 58
16. Ending mental prayer I 58
17. Ending mental prayer II 58
18. Prayer to God the Father 59
19. Prayer of Divine Mercy 61
20. Prayer of liberation against idolatry and superstition 63
21. Prayer for the poor souls in purgatory 65
22. Prayer of a family at the Nativity scene on Christmas 66
23. Prayer at the beginning of a pilgrimage to holy Land 68
24. Prayer to Christ in His Passion 70
25. Prayer to Christ in His Most Precious Blood 72
26. Prayer to the Holy Spirit I 75
27. Prayer to the Holy Spirit II 75
28. Spiritual Communion I 76
29. Spiritual Communion II 77
30. Spiritual Communion III 77
31. Visit to the Blessed Sacrament I 78
32. Visit to the Blessed Sacrament II 78

Prayers of the Soul

33.	Visit to the Blessed Sacrament III	79
34.	Visit to the Blessed Sacrament IV	79
35.	Visit to the Blessed Sacrament V	80
36.	Litany of a Sinner	80

II PRAYERS TO THE VIRGIN MARY, ANGELS AND SAINTS .. 85

37.	Act of consecration to Our Lady	87
38.	Prayer to Our Lady of Mount Carmel	87
39.	Prayer to the Most Holy Mother of God	88
40.	Prayer to Mary Most Holy Mother of God in her dogmas	89
41.	Prayer to the Immaculate Heart of Mary	91
42.	Prayer to the Virgin Mary in times of distress	93
43.	Prayer to our Sorrowful Mother	94
44.	Prayer to Saint Michael the Archangel	95
45.	Prayer to the Child Jesus	96
46.	Prayer to our Guardian Angel	97

III PRAYERS FOR PARTICULAR INTENTIONS ... 99

47.	Prayer for the Holy Father	101
48.	Prayer for priests	102
49.	Prayer for priests persecuted for defending the faith	103
50.	Prayer for priestly vocations	105
51.	Prayer for persecuted christians	106
52.	Prayer in the midst of the actual crisis in the Church	107
53.	Prayer for the evangelization of the peoples	109
54.	Prayer for christian unity	112
55.	Prayer for peace	114
56.	Prayer for immigrants	115
57.	Prayer for the sick	117
58.	Prayer of a mother for the conversion of her children	118
59.	Prayer for children suffering under extreme poverty	120
60.	Prayer for an extremely ill child	121
61.	Prayer for the death of a baptized child	122
62.	Prayer for the death of an unbaptized child	123
63.	Prayer for the end of abortion	125
64.	Prayer to be said outside the abortion chambers	126
65.	Prayer for the soul of someone who committed suicide	128
66.	Prayer for our enemies	130
67.	Prayer for our friends	130
68.	Prayer for intercession for those who ask to pray for them	131
69.	Prayer for creation	133
70.	Prayer for our Nation	134
71.	Prayer for the end of a pandemia	136

Table of Contents

IV PRAYERS IN PARTICULAR CIRCUMSTANCES 139
72. Prayer for employment 141
73. Prayer at the beginning of work 142
74. Prayer at the end of work 143
75. Prayer of a student..144
76. Prayer of blessing of a mother to her child 145
77. Prayer of a mother for a child with mental disabilities 145
78. Prayer for finding a good wife 147
79. Prayer for finding a good husband 148
80. Prayer of those who are engaged..........................150
81. Prayer of a married couple.....................................151
82. Prayer of a married couple in crisis 152
83. Prayer of divorced and remarried 154
84. Prayer of a pregnant woman 156
85. Prayer asking for fertility......................................157
86. Prayer of a widow 159
87. Prayer of a boy 161
88. Prayer of an altar boy...162
89. Prayer of a quinceañera (fifteen birthday)..........163
90. Prayer for perfect chastity 164
91. Prayer asking for discernment 166
92. Prayer for discerning a vocation 167
93. Prayer of a pastor or chaplain 168
94. Prayer of the catechumens 170
95. Prayer of the extraordinary ministers of Holy Communion.172
96. Prayer of the ministers of music during the Holy Mass ..173
97. Prayer of an artist..175
98. Prayer of a fallen away catholic............................176
99. Prayer asking for love of God 179
100. Prayer before driving 179
101. Prayer of the elderly 180
102. Prayer of the physician...182
103. Prayer before a surgery 183
104. Prayer of the sick 184
105. Prayer on a birthday..186
106. Prayer asking for final perseverance. 188
107. Prayer to know how to pray correctly 189
108. Prayer of humility I 190
109. Prayer of humility II 192
110. Prayer of Thanksgiving for a favor granted 193
111. Prayer of a prisoner 194
112. Prayer of those suffering from same sex attraction 196
113. Prayer of forgiveness of those who have offended us 198

114.	Prayer at the beginning of fasting	200
115.	Prayer of a penitent going to confession after many years	201
116.	Prayer of liberation from the sin of pride and arrogance	202
117.	Prayer of renunciation	205
118.	Prayer in time of loneliness	206
119.	Prayer during moments of anguish and anxiety	207
120.	Prayer for addiction deliverance	209
121.	Prayer to begin again after falling out from grace	210
122.	Prayer in moments of temptation of the flesh	213
123.	Prayer asking protection against the Devil	215
124.	Prayer in preparation for an imminent death	216

V EXTRA PRAYERS 221

125.	Prayer while taking off in an airplane	223
126.	Prayer before an important meeting	225
127.	Prayer of a police officer	226
128.	Prayer of healing for those who have been sexually abused	227
129.	Prayer of protection before a natural disaster	230
130.	Prayer of a soldier	231
131.	Prayer of a wife for the conversion of her husband	232
132.	Prayer before dinner on Thanksgiving	235
133.	Prayer to our Lady of Perpetual Help	236

VI PRAYERS TO THE GLORIOUS SAINT JOSEPH 239

134.	Prayer to Saint Joseph on the mysteries of his life.	241
135.	Prayer to Saint Joseph for the Church today	244
136.	Prayer of a husband to Saint Joseph	246
137.	Prayer to Saint Joseph during difficult times	247
138.	Prayer to Saint Joseph before leaving home	250
139.	Ave Saint Joseph.	251
140.	Prayer to Saint Joseph during a financial hardship	251
141.	Prayer to Saint Joseph asking for a holy death	252
142.	Family consecration through Saint Joseph	253
143.	Liliary to Saint Joseph	256
144.	Litanies to Saint Joseph	262

Preface

1. Prayer Life and Grace

Christian life is a life that is lived in a profound relationship with Christ and according to His mandates, but above all according to the action of His Divine Grace, without which we cannot do anything (cf. Jn 15: 5). But what is Grace? Grace is the life of God acting in us so we can be able to live according to the law of Christ with the purpose of achieving, through it, eternal life. But this life of grace that guides the entire Christian life is it not God's imposition on human beings against their freedom. No; in order to receive it, human beings must ask for it, work together with it, take care of it, increase it, and recover it, if it is lost at some point (cf. Phil 2:12). And this is why prayer is so important. Indeed, the totality of Christian life, which is a life of grace, obtains its oxygen, so to speak, from prayer. Through prayer, Christ inspires, calls, corrects, strengthens, and guides the believer to open himself to His grace. It is only by prayer, then, that a

Christian can cultivate a genuine relationship with God and thus enjoy the benefits of His grace.

The life of prayer can be compared to the life of someone who has fallen in love. In fact, those who are truly in love have a natural interest in being with the loved one in order to meet her (him), to know what she (he) likes and thus, please her (him). In the same way, in the relationship with God, which is a relationship of mutual love, prayer is constituted as an indispensable element. It consists of a constant search for God based on a profound desire to be with Him, to know Him better and thus to please Him. Through prayer, God ceases to be a simple concept and a cold abstraction. In it, God becomes a personal being who listens to us, someone to Whom we can speak, who knows our name, our history and who is interested in us, in our lives, in our joys and sorrows. In other words, through prayer God becomes a living and familiar God who continuously knocks at our door with the purpose of entering inside our souls and making in them His dwelling place (cf. Rev. 3:20).

2. Who does God listen to?

Now, how should our prayer be so that God not only listens to it, but rejoices in hearing it? There are two fundamental dispositions that we must take into account. The first is to experience a deep dependence on God, which is what the Gospel calls *"poverty of spirit"*, and the second disposition, deeply linked to the first, consists in being aware of our sinful and miserable condition before

Preface

a Holy God, who, nevertheless, is full of mercy and always willing and eager to listen to us.[1]

2.1. Dependence on God and spiritual poverty

If we look into Sacred Scripture in detail, we will find that those who are most likely to experience this

---

[1] It is important to clarify that the intention of this presentation is only to show two basic and primary dispositions during the time of prayer itself in order that our prayer be heard with pleasure by God. We do not intend, therefore, to exhaust here all the provisions that make prayer acceptable to God. It seems important to us, however, to point out the fundamental role that charity has in the life of prayer. Indeed, one cannot depend on God and recognize one's misery without, almost spontaneously and in parallel, feeling the urgency of putting one's life at the service of others, loving one's neighbor, especially those in most need. He who prays should never forget the words of the prophet Isaiah: *"Your novilunios and solemnities hate my soul: they have been a tax that I have trouble carrying. And as you extend your palms, I cover my eyes so as not to see you. Although you pray the prayer, I do not hear. Your hands are full of blood: wash yourselves, cleanse yourselves, take away your wrongdoing from my sight, give up doing evil, learn to do good, seek the right, give your rights to the oppressed, do justice to the orphan and the widow. Come, then, and let's dispute - says Yahweh-… ".* (Is 1:14 -18; cf. 59: 2). Charity is therefore basic, not only because it is a fundamental element to be pleasing to God, but because it is the main test about which we will be judged at the end of our lives (cf. Mt 25, 35-45). The reason we do not include charity among the provisions we point out here is because charity should be seen as a product of prayer, in everyday life and not so much, in the same act of praying. However, we can say that the act of praying for others is also an act of charity and love of neighbor and this is clear throughout this book, especially in Chapter III, where we present prayers in order to intercede for the needs of others.

dependence on God are the simple and the humble ones, that is, the poor, whom the Bible calls *anawin* (cf. Ps 33; Job 34: 28; 1 Sam 2: 8; Ps 102: 17. 107: 41). And why is this so? Because the poor know that everything they have, health, livelihood, possessions, etc. was received from God and in order not to lose these much needed possessions, they know they must remain with God praising Him, giving Him glory for His benefits and obeying His commandments (cf. Jn 9:31). Prayer is, in that sense, for the poor (*anawin*) not a luxury or a mystical extravagance, but their deepest necessity, not only spiritual, but material and even physical (cf. Ps 42). They come to God as a son approaches his father using words that are simple and familiar, but at the same time of deep love and respect (cf. 68: 5). Hence, in their material poverty they experience a special union with God Whom they need each day to live.

This dependence on God cannot, however, remain only on the purely material level. The poor must also depend on God on the spiritual and transcendental level. In order words, God must be everything for the *anawin* not only because He is the provider of their material needs, but above all because they find in Him the source of their life, their fulfillment, that is, the foundation on which everything depends, including their own happiness.

In the gospel of Matthew, Jesus talks about those who understand prayer in this way by proclaiming: *"Blessed are the poor in spirit"* (Mt 5, 3). Hence, being poor in the spirit goes beyond just being materially poor. Indeed, in the same way that the poor, materially speaking, live day by day procuring to satisfy their most basic needs from a source outside themselves, since they have no savings or wealth to rely on, likewise the poor in spirit know they are incapable of satisfying by themselves their hunger for eternal life. They need God and everything He can give them to achieve their spiritual happiness.

It is true that in order to possess this poverty of spirit, this dependence on God, it is certainly helpful to experience as well real poverty, it is to say, the knowledge of what it is like to live with limited material resources. However, it is also true that being poor - materially speaking - does not ensure *per se* this total dependence on God. In fact, there are poor people who live their lives away from God and dedicate themselves to theft, deceit, envy, and all kinds of injustices. On the other hand, there are rich people who, adorned with the beautiful virtue of humility, use their possessions in such a way that they are not attached to them, but on the contrary, consider that their greater profit is to use them to alleviate the misery of their neighbor. Such a people, though rich, live in a clear poverty of spirit.

We must never forget that God loves both: the rich and the poor, since He is the Creator of all (cf. Prov 22: 2) and that - as Saint Augustine said - the gift of poverty can be given to all kind of men living in all kinds of conditions since they can be equal through the desire for spiritual poverty. Even if they differ in wealth, this difference matters little if there is equality in the richness of the spirit. So, what really matters here is the interior disposition. A spirit that is poor is a spirit that is not self-sufficient, but in everything dependent on God. Who he is poor in spirit is aware of the difference between what in life is essentially important and necessary and what is secondary. This leads him to seek God and His justice first, knowing that everything else will be given in addition (cf. Mt 6:33). From this conviction comes the imperative need to pray and in doing so become pleasing to God. In that sense, both the poor (materially speaking) and the rich are capable of this spiritual poverty.

It is true that in the gospels, Jesus manifests a clear preference for the poor, but that does not mean that this preference excludes the rich just because they are rich. Let us remember that in Sacred Scripture, being rich is often a sign of having found favor in the eyes of God (cf. Gn 32: 10; Job 42: 12; Deut 15: 10; 1 Kg 3: 13). Indeed, Abraham, Job, David, Solomon, Hezekiah, and Joseph of Arimathea among others possessed riches at the same time that in their lives and in their prayer, they were pleasing to God. Likewise, in the history of the Church we find men and women who had a deep life of prayer while still preserving their wealth; such was the case of Saint Francis of Assisi, Saint Elizabeth of Hungary, Saint Stephen of Hungary and his son Saint Emeric, Saint Ladislaus and Saint Charles Borromeo, among others.

Now, it is true that for the rich, spiritual poverty requires more effort. In fact, when the rich, confused by the abundance of their wealth, put in it and not in God all their trust, they become incapable of this spiritual poverty. That is why God warns them *"and even if your wealth increases, do not give to it your hearts" (Ps 62: 10)*. Indeed, when the rich put their hope in the uncertainty of wealth and not in God (cf. 1 Tm 6: 17), they close themselves to the fruits of prayer (cf. Lk 16: 14-15; cf. 1 Tm 6: 10) since true prayer

Preface

is the only prayer that pleases God. The man who prays is required to have an absolute dependence on Him and His will. This is certainly impossible to do by somebody who has given himself to his possessions, putting his trust in them and not in God. As a result, God occupies a second place in his heart which leads him to believe himself eternal, losing sight of the fact that God could ask from him at any time the very life with which he plans to enjoy all his possessions: *"Fool! tonight I will claim your soul; the things you prepared, who will they be for?" (Lk 12: 20).*

For that reason, in order for the rich to be heard by God with delight, they must practice - as well as the poor - this absolute dependence on God, which consists in giving to Him a unique and exclusive place in their own heart. Therefore, those who expect God to be content by sharing the same place that their riches have cannot be heard. Lacking this dependence, the wealthy will not surrender themselves to God and instead will seek to establish with Him a relationship of equality, that of allies, of partners, but not of filial obedience. In a relationship where this dependence and this loving submission to God and His will are excluded, Christian prayer cannot take root.

The best example of this can be found in the rich young man of the gospel of Mathew, whom Christ deeply loved when He saw that his effort to live a good life was sincere, but who went away sad when Jesus asked him to leave everything and give it to the poor so that he would depend only on Him. When Jesus sees his response in his attitude, he exclaims: *"... it is very difficult for a rich man to enter the kingdom of heaven" (Mt 10: 17-30).* In other words, *"No one can serve two masters; because either he will hate the one and love the other, or he will esteem the one and despise the other. You cannot serve God and wealth" (Lk 16:13; Mt 6:24).*

In short, not only the poor, materially speaking, but also the rich can be poor in spirit and therefore their prayers can reach heaven and be pleasing to God. The poor achieve this by extending that material dependence they have from God to the spiritual realm because God must be everything to them. In the same way, also the rich can be "poor in spirit" as long as they do not turn their hearts to their riches and in their inner disposition live that profound dependence on God that recognizes Him as the only important and necessary good in this world, which in turn frees them from their material possessions that could turn them away from Him.

2.2. Humility and sincere recognition of our misery

The second step taken by the "poor in spirit" after recognizing their dependence on God is to acknowledge their misery before Him. As a consequence, they have a natural awareness that although God is willing to listen to them, He does so by His grace and goodness and not because of the virtue of the one who prays. The poor experience their unworthiness before God more directly since their material poverty helps them to be more aware of their sins and miseries. The need they have from God's help to achieve what they need to survive day by day teaches them to be humble, thus, to be more open and docile to submit themselves to His mandates and therefore, to recognize more easily when they transgress them. The rich, those who have not given their hearts to their riches, likewise, know very well that their possessions

Preface

are gifts from God and that in the end, they themselves in their miseries and weaknesses, and in their unworthiness before the presence of God, are not different from the rest of mortals (cf. Job 1:21).

The gospels offer us several examples in which we can observe, both in the rich and in the poor, that when we accept our weakness with humility, God listens to our prayer with great pleasure. Here we will point out only three of them: the tax collector (cf. Lk 18: 9-14), the Roman centurion (cf. Mt 8: 5-13) and the Canaanite woman (cf. 15: 21-28).

In the first case, Jesus tells us about two men praying in the temple: the first, a Pharisee and the second, a tax collector. *"The Pharisee stood by himself and prayed: 'God, I thank You that I am not like other people—robbers, evildoers, adulterers—or even like this tax collector. I fast twice a week and give a tenth of all I get'" (Lk 18: 11-12).* Once the Pharisee finished his prayer, returned home without being heard by God, since he lacked humility, which is nothing other than the deep awareness of who we are before God. Very different was the attitude of the tax collector who, knowing he was a sinner, was aware that he did not deserve to be heard by God, which is why he did not dare to gaze to the heavens, but on the contrary, from afar, while striking his chest, prayed: *"Oh God! Have mercy on me, I am a sinner!"* (18: 13). God accepted the tax collector's prayer and was pleased with Him. The Lord ends this example with the following words: *"For everyone who exalts himself will be humbled; and he who humbles himself will be exalted"* (v.14).

In the second example, we see the Roman centurion approaching Jesus with the intention to ask Him to heal his servant. At this request, Jesus offers to go immediately. The centurion, however, knows that if Jesus enters his house, He will be contaminated (the Jews could not enter the house of a gentile without being contaminated). That is why the centurion tells Jesus: *"Lord, I am not worthy that You shall enter under my roof; but just say the word and my servant will be healed"* (Mt 8: 8). These words filled Jesus with a singular admiration which made Him exclaim: *"I assure you that in Israel I have not found in anyone such a great faith"* (v. 10). Jesus not only healed the centurion's servant, but rejoiced in his humility and faith. The Church, aware of Jesus' positive reaction to hearing these words of the centurion, incorporated them into her liturgy and placed them just before the reception of Holy Communion as an expression of deep faith and humility that pleases God greatly.

Finally, we have the case of the Canaanite woman, a foreigner, who approaches Jesus begging Him to free her daughter from the power of the devil who possessed her. Jesus, however, seems to ignore her. Even the disciples tried to pressure Him in attending to her petitions, not so much for consideration towards the woman, but for her insistence which had begun to annoy them: *"Listen to her that she is shouting behind us"* (15: 23). But Jesus insists on His refusal to listen to her, because according to Him, *"I have been sent only to the lost sheep of the house of Israel"* (v. 24). The foreign woman, however, does not give up and prostrating before Him pleads: *"Lord help me!"* To which Jesus responds: *"It is not right to take the children's bread and throw it to the little dogs"* (v. 26). Perhaps

Preface

another woman would have felt offended in her pride upon hearing these harsh words of Jesus and would have withdrawn disappointed away from the Teacher. But not this woman, who with great humility responded: *"Yes, Lord; but also, the dogs eat of the crumbs that fall from the table of their masters"* (v. 27). Jesus heard her prayer and praised her great faith saying: *"Woman great is your faith; Let it happen to you as you wish"* (v. 28).

The Lord has come for all, but first it was necessary to offer His salvation to Israel; the people of the covenant, the pagans had to wait their turn. It is clear that Jesus was putting this woman to a test, since as we have seen, to the centurion he did agree to help him immediately, despite the fact that he was a pagan too. But in this case, Jesus intended to test the humility of the non-Jewish woman to the limit in order to see if she was worthy to be heard. The Canaanite woman humbled herself and accepted her place in the plan of salvation; she recognized that Jesus did not have to listen to her, therefore her insistence was not based on the claim of a right, but on a humble hope in the goodness and kindness of the Master. This attitude pleased Jesus very much and that is why he granted what she asked for, the release of her little girl from the power of the devil.

This same disposition that we find in the gospels is also found throughout the history of the Church in the lives of the saints. Indeed, they also teach us that in order to make God listen to us with pleasure, it is necessary for us to humble ourselves before Him. Indeed, the saints were very clear about who they were and who this God Whom they served was. For that reason, they always kept these words in mind: *"For he who exalts himself will be humbled, and he who humbles himself will be exalted"* (Lk 18:14). As a consequence, the saints saw others as more worthy than themselves (cf. Phil 2: 3); and if they did so with mere mortals, with greater reason they did it with God. Let us remember that St. Peter, for example, who after witnessing the miracle of the fish, prostrated himself before Jesus exclaiming: *"Get away from me, Lord, for I am a sinful man"* (cf. Lk 5: 8); or St. Paul, who never let himself be daunted by anyone when he had to defend his rights, but when it came to his call before God, he considered himself abnormally born, the most insignificant of all the apostles (cf. 1 Cor 15: 8-9).

St Augustine, the doctor of grace, also opens his "Confessions" in this way:

> *"Great art thou, O Lord, and greatly to be praised; great is thy power, and infinite is thy wisdom." And man desires to praise thee, for he is a part of thy creation; he bears his mortality about with him and carries the evidence of his sin and the proof that thou dost resist the proud."*

Thomas à Kempis author of the Christian classic *"The Imitation of Christ"* addresses God with these words:

> *"O sweet and loving Lord, (…) You know my weakness and the need that I suffer, by how many evils and vices I am overwhelmed, it is not hidden to You of how many times I have been overwhelmed, tempted, disturbed and stained by my sins. I come to You for remedy, to You I go for comfort and relief (…) You know the goods that I most need, and how poor I am in virtues."*

Preface

Likewise, the great Spanish mystic Saint Teresa of Jesus addresses God in one of her songs saying: *"I am Yours and for You I was born, what do You want of me? Majestic Sovereign, Unending wisdom, Kindness pleasing to my soul; God sublime, one Being Good, behold this one so vile. Singing of her love to You: What do You want of me?"*

Also, St. Alphonsus Liguori exclaims, addressing the Virgin Mary:
"The Eternal one fell in love with your incomparable beauty, with such a force, that He decided to leave the Father's bosom to come to your virginal womb to become your Son. And I, earthly worm, shouldn't I love you? Yes, my sweet Mother, I want to burn in your love for you and I propose to exhort others to love you as well."

Finally, St. Francis Solano choses a similar adjective to describe himself: *"Who are You, Lord, and my God, who am I a vile earthworm!"* Similar quotations can be found by the millions throughout the spiritual writings of the saints.

For the modern man, so friendly to highlight only the positive and the greatness of human nature, hearing these adjectives with which the saints used to refer to themselves in the presence of God, could be incomprehensible and even scandalous. But this attitude of the saints did not respond to a pessimistic notion about human nature, much less does it respond to a false humility. It was, rather, a natural and spontaneous disposition resulting from a true conversion that made these men and women understand who they were before God. They did not ignore the greatness and the beauty with which they were fashioned by the hands of their

Creator; yet they knew they also were fallen creatures, always in need of Divine Grace. It was this clear awareness of their poor condition that made God not only listen to them, but be pleased with their prayers and thus crown them with holiness.

In conclusion, dependence on God and humility in recognizing one's misery are the two main dispositions needed to secure a deep relationship with God. Without them there can be no progress, neither in the life of grace, nor in the life of prayer. Both express the ability to recognize that my existence depends entirely on God and that because of my human and sinful condition; I am unworthy to stand before Him. In spite of this, God loves me and has bowed down graciously to listen to me.

When the believer experiences these two fundamental aspects of his relationship with God in the depths of his soul, prayer becomes for him an indispensable element of his life. For that reason, following the advice of the Apostle, the believer prays incessantly (cf. 1 Thes 5:17) and does so in moments of consolation, joy, and abundance, to intercede for others who are in need, but also and especially in those moments of darkness, need and misfortune. And it is especially in these last moments that prayer acquires a deeper and more mysterious meaning.

3. Prayer and suffering

When we pray the prayer of the Hail Holy Queen we say: *"To you do we cry, poor banished children of Eve; to you do we send up our sighs, mourning and weeping in this valley of tears"*. By praying in this way, we confess that human life takes place in this world in a state of exile. Although there are moments of happiness and joy in this life, our condition is always of transit, not only of material goods, but of life itself which is constantly threatened by misfortune, pain, suffering and even death. This happens either because of the very nature of life, or as a consequence of our sins and miseries, and it is from this reality that our need and our dependence on God becomes even stronger.

We will never be totally happy in this world as long as we do not have God fully, which cannot happen in this life, but only after death. In this context, prayer plays a fundamental role in our life. Indeed, as pilgrims on this earth in the midst of needs and sufferings, we need prayer to unite us more to God and to open for Him the doors of our souls. In this way, He can work much more effectively in procuring our spiritual growth by helping us to know Him better and therefore be better disposed to work out our own salvation (cf. Phil 2:12).

Let us remember the case of Job in whom God took pleasure while living in the abundance, but who demonstrated his true love and faith in God only when he lost everything. It was in these moments of pain and suffering that Job learned to distinguish what is secondary and auxiliary from what is truly important and permanent in life. Likewise, the suffering caused by painful experiences in life guides the believer to find refuge in prayer. Through prayer, the true disciple grows more in faith and renews his trust in God by understanding that the true meaning of this life lies not in itself, nor in its goods, but in finding in God and in His will the ultimate meaning of human existence.

These moments of suffering are, by their very nature, moments that reveal what is really and deeply human, moments in which the human heart can experience, more than in times of happiness, the vulnerability and fragility of its condition. Moments so profoundly human as these are also moments so richly filled with the presence of God. In fact, the closer we are to God, the more we become really and truly human, freed from facades and pretensions. God better than anybody knows and understands the weakness, vulnerability, and tiredness of the one who suffers, because only through suffering men can realize who they really are and who God really is on Whom they totally depend to be happy.

In that sense, God not only allows, but expects that in prayer, the believer naturally expresses all his weaknesses and miseries, including the great mystery of feeling sometimes *"abandoned by God."* Sacred Scripture contains extremely difficult passages where in the face of suffering, the believer expresses his sentiments before God with radical crudeness. For example, in the midst of suffering Job exclaims:

> *"May the day of my birth perish, and the night that said, 'A boy is conceived!' That day—may it turn to darkness; may God above not care about it; may no light shine on it. May gloom and utter darkness claim it once more; may a cloud settle over it; may blackness overwhelm it. That night—may thick darkness seize it; may it not be*

Preface

included among the days of the year nor be entered in any of the months" (Job 3: 3-6).

Or even the words spoken by Jesus Himself from the cross: *"My God, my God, why have You forsaken me?"* (Ps 21: 1; Mt 27: 46). God does not reject these deeply human expressions in times of suffering, but instead accompanies us, comforts us, and gives us hope in order to help us persevere and be able, at some point in our process, to praise and thank Him for His fidelity. Indeed, the Psalm 22, cited above, used by Jesus from the cross to express His pain and abandonment, ends as follows: *"And I will live for the LORD; my descendants will serve You. The generation to come will be told of the Lord, that they may proclaim to a people yet unborn the deliverance You have brought...."* (22: 31-32). Thus, these moments of difficulty are transformed through prayer into opportunities, not so much to show God what we will do, but above all to know ourselves how much we love God and how willing we are to let God be God in our own lives, knowing that he who trusts in the Lord will never be disappointed (cf. Rom 10:11).

Prayer, made in these circumstances gives the believer great peace and deep joy in discovering that this God, in Whom he has put all his trust, to Whom he has submitted himself with filial love, and from Whom he has accepted His will, whatever it may be, is a God so personal and so close that He walks and suffers with him at all times. Indeed, He is not a God who, from a distance in a cold and indifferent way, observes how His will is imposed on His creature. No; the Christian God is a God who engages in the drama of our lives in a real way - a God who listens and suffers with us -. How could the believer lose hope in the midst of suffering when he knows he is being accompanied by such a God? It is in the hands of this good, close, and personal God in Whom lies the totality of our lives and in whose judgment, we have full confidence, that we entrust the entirety of our beings, to such an extent, that we Christians can exclaim with Job: *"The Lord gave it to me, the Lord took it away, blessed be the name of the Lord"* (Job 1:21).

But if this God is truly God, who knows what is best for me and thus asks from me faithful obedience to His will, then why shall we pray? What can our prayer do? St. Augustine tells us that we do not pray to inform God of something He does not know, instead we pray out of our own need to tune in to His will and thus be able to receive what God offers us. It is an exercise of conversion, of transformation of who we are. When we experience pain, suffering, illness, the burden of our own limitations, as well as the limitations of others, we place ourselves in His hands, and let ourselves be educated by His will. We are trained into thinking like Him, in order to see things as He sees them and finally, learn not only to accept His will, but actually to desire that everything in this life has the outcome He wants.

4. "Lord, teach us how to pray" (Lc 11: 1)

But how do we know what God wants from us? What is it that we should ask for and how? The disciples had this same concern and humbly turned to Jesus saying: *"Lord, teach us to pray as John taught his disciples"* (Lk 11: 1). The good Teacher, then, taught them the Our Father, the Christian prayer par excellence. This prayer is, indeed, the example of every prayer because it comes from God

Himself, and no one better than Him knows what we need to ask; but also because in it all these elements necessary to establish a true relationship with God, and which we have mentioned before, are present. The Our Father teaches us not to ask for what we think we need, but what we should ask, in what order we should ask for it, and what is the attitude with which we should raise our request. This attitude is humility. God teaches us to pray and helps us to do so to the point that He gives us the exact words with which to address Him, because He knows that we do not know how to ask as we should (cf. Rom 8: 26).

The Our Father is not only a formula, but a way of life, a spirituality, a school of prayer based on these two provisions to which we have referred earlier, that is, dependence on God and recognition of one's own misery. Indeed, in the Our Father we see very clearly this dependence because we are told to call Him "Abba," "Daddy," which is a unique and new way of addressing God, hence, fulfilling what we have said before, that this dependence is not from an abstract God, but from a concrete and personal one who loves us and cares about us just like a father does with his son. In this prayer, God teaches us to praise Him first of all, to ask for the coming of His kingdom, to live according to His will, and to ask for our material support. Next, the Lord's Prayer teaches us to recognize our misery: *"forgive us our sins because we also forgive everyone who has sinned against us ..."* (Lk 11: 4) He is, in that sense, a God who is so personal that He expects reciprocity: *"I will forgive you your sins, but only if you forgive those who offended you."* Finally, it teaches us to ask to be delivered from evil and sin, which although may gain for us the whole world, makes us lose our souls, God and His grace.

The Our Father taught by Jesus to His disciples as a concrete way to address God does not, however, exclude the fact that we can at all times speak with God in our own words. After all - as Saint Teresa of Avila said - prayer is nothing more than cultivating a friendship with Him who loves us. Spontaneous, or discursive, prayer is, in that sense, not only important, but indispensable in the Christian life. Yet, in order to be able to address God with a spontaneous prayer, this must be born from the truth about God and man. That is why He wants, first, to show us how to pray by giving us a paradigm of prayer to inspire and form our personal and spontaneous prayer. Otherwise, there is a risk that our prayer can become something merely subjective and individualistic, unrooted and divorced from what God has shown us about Himself.

5. Faith and Vocal Prayer

To free our relationship with God from the danger of subjectivity, Christian prayer must be formed by faith, faith not only as trust in God *fides qua*, but as content *fides quae*. In other words, it is good to trust God, but who is this God Whom I trust? What does He think and what does He expect of me? It is here that my prayer must find its inspiration in the Word of God and in the Liturgy. *Lex credendi, Lex orandi.*[2] My way of praying, without losing its spontaneity, must be fed by my faith, from what I believe.

---

[2] Literally it means the law of faith is the law of prayer. In other words, in the liturgy, prayer must reflect that which we believe.

Preface

A Christian's prayer cannot be the same as a Buddhist or a Muslim prayer or a simple meditation. As we have pointed out so far, in Christian prayer, the believer addresses God, but not an *absconditus*[3], impersonal or abstract God, neither a subjective, relativistic God, made according to our image and likeness. No, we Christians address a God who has revealed Himself, who has spoken and intervened in history, and consequently, all of this must be perceived in the way we address Him. A Christian, in that sense, never prays alone, nor isolated, but as a member of the Church, that is, inserted into a history and tradition. That is why every personal prayer must be, in a sense, an echo and an extension of the Church's prayer.

This is the origin and greatness of vocal prayer. Vocal prayer is the most elementary form of Christian prayer. It is one that we memorize or read and pronounce audibly or mentally. This form of prayer constitutes the most common way of prayer of the simple people, of the multitudes. According to Saint Teresa, this prayer is made interior as we become aware of the One to *"Whom we speak"* (cf. CCC # 2704). For its part, the Catechism teaches us that vocal prayer is the first form of

---

[3] Deus absconditus is a term which appears in Isaiah 45: 15 to express the greatness and transcendence of God. The correct sense of understanding lies in that God cannot be fully known by mere understanding; in that sense it is a God who hides. The term, however, acquired a new meaning when it was used by deism which - along with the term Deus otiosus - sought to express the idea of a God who creates the world and disregards it. It is then a hidden, distant, and indifferent God before human suffering. In this sense, Deus abcondritus is not the Christian God and that is how it is used here.

contemplative prayer (cf. # 2708), which allows us to say that vocal prayer is the first step for spontaneous prayer, which not for the fact of being spontaneous prayer, which does not cease to be vocal prayer in itself from the fact that it is spontaneous prayer. Jesus Himself endorsed this type of prayer when he addressed His Father several times (cf. Jn 17: 1-15). In another part, He instructed His disciples in this type of prayer by teaching them the vocal prayer par excellence, the Our Father. Moreover, in several opportunities He shared with them the prayer of the Psalms (cf. Mt 26:30).

Our parents and grandparents, imitating this gesture of Jesus with His disciples, taught us as children to memorize prayers such as the "Our Father", the "Hail Mary", the "I confess", the "Act of contrition" or the "Guardian Angel", etc. All these vocal prayers sought to train us in dealing with God, using simple words but full of faith. Thus, just as a child begins to walk guided by the hand of his mother, so also, through these prayers, our parents planted the foundations of a true relationship with God.

In this context, the word *"relationship"* - which is what vocal prayer wants to establish between God and us- has a special connotation. In fact, in Christian theology, when we talk about a relationship with God, it should always be understood that this relationship occurs in the context of a reestablishment of this relationship. A recurring theme not only in Christianity, but in all religions, is this constant search to reestablish our relationship with God, a relationship that was broken at a certain moment in history by the fault of man, which is

Preface

what we call in Catholic theology, original sin. Only in Christianity, in the person of Christ, has this relationship been fully restored.

The Catholic Church is, in that sense, the extension in time of this restoration, making it available in her bosom to all men, which is why she constitutes herself as the one true religion. Religion is a word that comes from the Latin *re-ligare*, which means being united again with God; in other words, in the Catholic Church the true and only way to be reunited with God can be found. Thus, through Christian prayer - born of the Church's prayer – human beings are able to re-establish and re-encounter this God from Whom they had departed. Vocal prayer, totally imbued in the Catholic spirit, that is, in Christian revelation, helps the believer to re-encounter the true and only God, but as part of a redeemed humanity.

All of the above makes us understand a very important dimension in the crisis that afflicts the Church today. Indeed, a growing number of Catholics of the new generations, indifferent and even adverse in practicing the Catholic religion, manifest their intentions to seek God outside the limits of the true religion, in practices that "free" them from a personal God who has intervened in history, who has shown His face and communicated His will to us. Thus, they are attracted rather by the so-called "Eastern spiritualities" which present an impersonal god, who cannot love and who is not interested in our concrete life. It is, therefore, a divinity as a force, as energy to which the human being, in his eagerness to escape from this world, seeks to be part of - or more properly said - to merge to the point of losing his own self, producing in the process an immediate feeling of "freedom". It is a kind of "third way", where reason and faith lose their hegemonic role to give way and priority to intuition, imagination, emotion, or atonement of consciousness, where the body has a leading role.

It is, then, a Gnostic conception of God. This is why yoga, reiki and taichí, just to name a few examples, have become so popular in our day. These practices are inseparable from the spiritualities or philosophies that originated them, such as Hinduism, Shintoism, Animism and the "new age", which exclude the existence of a personal God and focus on individuals. Unfortunately, today, there are not a few Catholics who have fallen into these errors, due to a deep lack of true religion as well as a lack of training in vocal prayer, whose foundations were not properly placed, or worse, were totally absent during childhood.

6. "Prayers of the soul"

It is in this context that this book entitled *"Prayers of the Soul"* wants to provide a service. It is a collection of one hundred and forty written prayers to worship God, honor the saints, ask for different intentions, as well as in various personal and difficult circumstances, in order to help those who want to pray, but do not know how, or cannot find the right words. This work is written for all, but it is directed especially for the laity, the common Christian, who lives in the world and who, to meet his personal needs and those of his family, is immersed in a number of occupations in the midst of which they may find it difficult to set aside time for personal prayer.

Preface

These prayers want to be a help so that wherever they find themselves, they can address God with the right words in their circumstances or specific needs. Moreover, they are prayers that are presented in a simple way, but at the same time are deeply inspired by Holy Scripture and the faith of the Church. Its composition seeks not only to facilitate prayer, but to nourish the faith and knowledge of God of the one who prays, by taking him out of his comfort zone and challenging him to grow into a more mature faith. Some are very short and concrete, others - longer in length – have the intention to be, rather than simple formulas, a way to bring the heart of the person who prays to conversion, meditation and contemplation in a truly Christian way.

This book also intends to be a medicine of sound doctrine in an environment like the one in which we live today of a profound confusion. In fact, the believer never expresses his faith more clearly than when he prays, and that is why prayer becomes stronger and more mature when it is imbued by faith. Thus, this book is a loud cry that *"the Catholic faith, believed everywhere, forever and for all"*[4] is, unlike what many today believe, the answer and the

---

[4] This phrase "Quod ubique quod semper quod ab omnibus creditum est" is found in the Commonitorium or Conmonitorio, treaty written in the 5th century after the Council of Ephesus (431) and attributed to St. Vincent de Lerins, father of the Church. In this work, St. Vincent set out to facilitate, with examples of the Tradition and the history of the Church, the criteria to keep the Catholic truth intact. The method to preserve this truth is - according to St. Vincent - very simple and accessible to all believers, even the simplest, who in case of any doubt or in times of deep confusion recommends holding on to what, in the Church, has been believed by everyone, always and everywhere.

medicine for all the diseases and difficulties of our lives. No matter how dark, how terrible, how far from God our lives seem to be, *"De profundis"* from the depths (cf. Ps 130) we can always cry out to God, steadfast in our glorious Catholic faith (2 Thes 2:15).

Indeed, the solution to our different needs and circumstances is neither fleeing from the truth, inventing a god that does not exist, nor making God say things He never said with the goal of "feeling" good. The true solution in difficult moments of life, the true comfort in moments of darkness and sufferings, is in embracing with our whole being the true faith in the only God, in order to know what He expects of us in those difficult moments of our life. A "pastoral approach" and a "spirituality" that teaches us to deal with a false god, no matter how well it makes us "feel," is a deception destined to fail.

In this little book, the reader will find prayers that are in themselves also small "creeds", "professions of faith" whose goal is to comfort us and console us in the truth about what the good God wants from us in our concrete circumstances. In praying with them we do not turn to an abstract god, but to the true God, to the God who has revealed Himself, who has shown us His face and communicated the terms of the relationship He wants to establish with us.

All these prayers have been written with the awareness of the elements that we have been mentioning and that constitute the soul of Christian prayer. That is, the dependence of the believer on God, the awareness of the poverty and misery of the soul before God, and finally,

Preface

the greatness of this God who despite all of this, loves us and wants to listen to us. The purpose of these prayers is to help the soul to address God with humility, in order to achieve what is requested. It is thus seeking to make our prayer more like that of the tax collector and not that of the Pharisee, a constant danger in the life of prayer. This work wants to be, then, more than a book, a path, an itinerary, a moment of transformation. In short, it is meant to be a pedagogy of faith that transforms us internally and forges holiness in us while we ask God for what we need.

We are sure that for those who seek God, who want to love Him, know Him, and be transformed by His grace, this book will be very helpful. It will become an excellent companion, not only in the parish, in the chapel of Eucharistic adoration, in a retreat or in the prayer group, but also at home, on the night table, on the office desk, in the glove compartment of the car, in short, in the daily life of every Christian.

In the same way that Jesus proposed to His disciples the Our Father in response to the request to *"Teach us to pray"* (Lk 11: 1), so also, this little work, wants to be an answer for those who, in our time, have the eagerness of meeting the true God in prayer, but do not know how. Through it, the reader will discover that in all circumstances, no matter how dark it may seem, we can always cry out to God for our benefit and for the benefit of others, with the conviction that, if we do it with the correct disposition, He will listen to us. May these prayers open wide the hearts of those who dispose themselves through them to converse with God. May God listen propitious to all who make them their own and who can, helped by them, reach the summits of the spiritual life, which occurs when God is welcomed to dwell into our humble souls through the power of His grace. *"Behold, I stand at the door and knock. If anyone hears my voice and opens the door, I will enter his house and dine with him, and he with me"* (Rev. 3:20).

Father Juan Carlos Gavancho
June 30th, 2019
Feast of the Roman Martyrs of the Church of Rome

I DAILY PRAYERS AND DEVOTIONS DIRECTED TO GOD

Prague, Czech Republic. The baroque painting of Holy Trinity in church kestrel Svatého Tomáše by Karel Škréta (1610 - 1674).

I Daily Prayers and Devotions directed to God

1. Morning prayer

Lord Jesus, King, and Sun of justice, You have risen to illuminate the entire world with the radiance of Your glorious resurrection. I thank You for this day that now begins. I humbly receive it as a new opportunity that I do not deserve.

Help me, I beseech You, to live this day without losing Your grace and in deep communion with You, in such a way that there would not be in me, act, thought, sentiment, impulse, desire, inspiration or effort that does not find You as its source and its summit.

Help me to be, for all those with whom I will have contact today, a faithful sign of Your love, of Your patience, of Your solicitude. Do not let me - not even for a minute - succumb to temptation, and help me to arrive to night, still as Your friend, as a son of God, and as an inviolate temple of the Holy Spirit.

Give me the wisdom to always promote peace among those around me, but never at the cost of refusing or compromising Your Word. May I prefer death, Lord, before betraying the faith that I received from Your holy Church, my Mother.

Let me not forget, not even for a second, that You have given me this day filled with grace with the only purpose to save my soul and cooperate in the salvation of those who today You will put in my path. At the beginning of this day, I take Your hand and the hand of Your Blessed Mother, holy Mary, morning star. Amen.

2. Night prayer I

Lord of hope, God of forgiveness and clemency, I thank You for this day that Your goodness has brought to its completion. All the good that I found in it are gifts of Your love, all the bad things opportunities to improve mine.

Today I humbly accept that I failed You and that is why I come before You to ask for Your forgiveness. I could have been more patient, and I lost my temper. I could have been more prudent, and I took a chance. I could have been more generous, and I was selfish. I could have been more charitable, and I preferred myself. I could have sacrificed more, and I looked only for my pleasure. I could have worked harder but I chose to waste my time.

Having asked for Your forgiveness and confident that in Your goodness You will forgive me, I am determined to be a better person tomorrow. I will close my eyes now thinking only of You and when I wake up tomorrow, Lord, it is my fervent desire that You also be the one who occupies the first of my thoughts. And if in Your wisdom You decide that this shall be my last night on this earth, grant me the grace, O God of love and tenderness, of a holy death.

In the company of Your Holy Mother and mine as well, Mary, Queen of heaven, good night my Lord and my God. Amen. *(One Our Father, three Hail Marys and a Glory Be ...).*

I Daily Prayers and Devotions directed to God

3. Night Prayer II

Almighty God, at the end of this day when darkness fills the face of the earth, I want to thank You for all that I lived today. For all the good things You gave me and for the good things You allowed me to do.

But I also humbly want to implore forgiveness from You. How weak and how fragile I am, Lord. You are everything and I, who am I, Lord, without You? Absolutely nothing, and behold, nothing has rebelled against the one who is everything.

I am so sorry for breaking Your commandments, I am so sorry for despising Your beatitudes, I am so sorry for not waiting on Your promises and I am heartly sorry for not loving You as You love me. I have failed You, Lord, have mercy on me.

It is time to close my eyes, but I do not want to do it without knowing that You forgive me, without receiving Your mercy and without asking You to give me another chance tomorrow. I promise You that I will do my best to respond better to Your grace, much better than what I did today. Amen.
(One Our Father, three Hail Maryes and a Glory Be ...).

4. Act of contrition

Jesus, Son of the Most High, most beloved God and Lord of my life, I have failed You; I have betrayed You and I have denied You.

My will arose against You who have only given me good things. Of these good things that You have given me, I have used to offend You. For this, I should justly deserve Your condemnation. It is so, that if I were to die at this very moment it will be in conformity with justice for You to send my soul forever to eternal damnation.

But You are good, Lord, and among those gifts that Your grace has given me, and continues to give me, is the gift of time, through which, although it is true, I offended You, today I can, contrite and humble, implore Your forgiveness.

Behold I place myself before Your majesty, O Good and Merciful God, have mercy on me and forgive me. I ask this from You with deep humility, I do not deserve to be called Your son (daughter) anymore (cf. Lk 15:21). But if You accept me, Lord, and forgive me I promise You the following: to avoid near occasions of sin, to make a good sacramental confession, and to pray more intensely so that never, Good Lord, never again, will I dare to hurt Your loving heart. Amen.

5. Prayer before the Holy Mass I

Lord Jesus, God of love and consolation, I thank You for giving me the opportunity to come to Your holy house and participate in this Holy Mass. I beg You to

I Daily Prayers and Devotions directed to God

help me to live this moment with the same spirit with which the saints lived it. Deliver me from all distractions, that only of You and in no one but You may I think during this time. Remove all bad and idle thoughts from me. Forgive any venial sin or any imperfection that I may have in my soul. Open my ears to hear Your Word and let me be transformed by it. Open my eyes so that in the bread and the wine, after being consecrated by the blessed hands of Your priest, I may recognize Your Body and Your Blood.

May I always value the holy Mass and never treat it superficially, that I may always understand that this great mystery of faith does not belong to me or to this particular community, but to the Universal Church. This holy Mass is the sacred actualization of Your holy sacrifice that is the cause of the salvation of mankind. Grant that this Eucharist may fill my heart with love for You and for my brothers whom You ask me to serve.

On Your holy Altar I place every member of my family, for their offenses and for mine own, I entreat You to grant forgiveness. Help me to faithfully stay by Your side just like Your mother, Mary Most Holy, did at the foot of the cross. Under her maternal care I place myself during this great celebration of Your love for me and for the whole world. Amen.

6. Prayer before Holy Mass II

Jesus, You are the Lamb of God who takes away the sins of the world, I am about to participate in Your wedding feast, which is Your holy sacrifice in which You have redeemed all mankind (cf. Rev 19: 90). I humbly ask You to help me live in the best possible way every moment of this holy Mass. That my heart be prepared to welcome You; that my mind be aware at every moment of what is really happening. Deliver me from the temptation to seek in this Holy Mass entertainment, protagonism or superficiality. I come here as the deer comes to drink from the waters of Your salvation (cf. Ps 41). I confess, therefore, that this sacrifice is the same one that You carried out two thousand years ago, on the wood of the cross, and that it is now present on the altar, although this time in a bloodless fashion.

I firmly believe that during the consecration, the bread and the wine will be transformed by the power of the Holy Spirit through the consecrated hands of Your priest, into Your Body and into Your Blood and then offered to God, the Father, for the salvation of my soul.

I ask You, Lord, that the Holy Mass that I will now attend be celebrated according to the spirit of the liturgy, faithfully respecting the proper rubrics of the Latin rite and that Your Word, Your Body, and Your Blood be treated with the greatest respect, since it is You Yourself, sweet Lord Jesus, who are adored in heaven by angels and saints. May You be always loved and adored by every

I Daily Prayers and Devotions directed to God

creature in the face of this earth and in the highest heavens. Amen.

7. Prayer after the Holy Mass I

I thank You, Lord of heaven and earth, for giving me the great gift of participating in Your heavenly feast here on earth. I thank You for meeting with my brothers and sisters, for feeding me with Your holy Word, and for listening to our prayers for the Church and for the whole world. I thank You, too, for allowing me to contemplate Your saving work through the hands of the priest and for witnessing Your descent to this world in the simplicity of bread and wine.

I thank You, my God, because I have received You in my soul through Holy Communion and I thank You also for welcoming You now into my heart which rejoices without measure. Help me, then, to be a faithful dwelling place of Your holy presence, never allow me to leave You. Wherever I go, come with me and in the moments of darkness remind me that You are within me and that I need only this to overcome all the snares of the evil one. Amen.

8. Prayer after the Holy Mass II

Lord, my King and my God, I thank You immensely for the sacrifice of the holy Mass in which You have allowed me to partake.

The greatest thing in this world, what many prophets and kings wanted to see, and did not see, wanted to hear and did not hear (cf. Lk 10:24), You have allowed me, poor and miserable sinner as I am, to contemplate with my own eyes, that is, the salvation of the entire world through the sacrifice of Your cross. Help me to internalize each word, to meditate in each gesture and to be aware of every reality that I have witnessed today.

I humbly ask Your divine assistance so that my faith can grow even more and my life may be born, be centered and oriented towards the unfathomable mystery of Your love, presented ineffably in the holy Mass. Fill me with love for You and may this pledge of the future glory that I have received today help me to achieve the beauty of Your glory in heaven, once You, in Your goodness and wisdom, decide to end my human trajectory in this valley of tears. Amen.

9. Prayer after sacramental confession

Father Most holy, God of love and forgiveness, I thank You for receiving me with open arms in Your holy house (cf. Lk 15: 20). I got lost once again, Lord, I strayed from Your path, committing the evil that You hate (cf. Ps 50: 4), but behold, Your grace moved me to repentance and inspired me to return to the bosom of the Church, my mother.

I Daily Prayers and Devotions directed to God

In her, You have deposited the fruits of redemption and the forgiveness of sins. Upon receiving this sacrament of reconciliation, I firmly believe that You, Lord, have forgiven me and welcomed me again as Your son (daughter). All the sins I have confessed to the priest, no matter how terrible they were, no longer exist, they have been consumed by the holy fire of Your love and Your mercy.

I firmly believe all this, Lord, and for that reason my heart rejoices exceedingly, and I thank You. Help me; I beseech You, to strive every day to avoid the near occasion of sin and to never offend You again, betraying thus Your confidence and Your tenderness. Thank You, Lord, God of love and infinite mercy *"... I am Your servant, the son of Your slave, You have released my chains"* (Ps 116: 16). Amen. (*Now we pray the penance imposed by the priest*).

10. Prayer of consecration to the Heart of Jesus

Sweet and loving Heart of Jesus, before You I prostrate myself with deep humility and profoundly ashamed of how much I have offended Your Divine Heart. I am confident though in how much You have loved me and in the grace You have placed at my disposal.

Kindly accept on this day, I ask You, the offering of myself: my body, my soul, my will, my freedom and each of my thoughts, affections, intentions, works and even my passions, everything that

Prayers of the Soul

I am, and I possess, all my projects and my dreams, all my present, my past and my future, all that I am. Lord, take it. It is Yours.

Accept it as a poor offering placed with devotion in front of Your sovereign majesty, as a modest tribute to Your Heart pierced by my offenses, which is never tired of loving and forgiving me.

Accept me, O Lord, as a propitiation for all the outrages, offenses, insults, sacrileges, and indifferences to which Your Sacred Heart is exposed every day, in every corner of the world, not only by the enemies of Your kingdom, but even by those who vowed to serve You at one point in their lives.

Your Heart was pierced by the spear, and from it Blood and Water sprouted, in this same Divine Heart I take refuge. May that Water purify me and may that Blood protect me and thus I consecrate myself to You, O Kind Father, accept me and dispose of me according to Your most holy will. Amen.

11. Prayer of the priest before Holy Mass.

Lord Jesus, high Priest, and holy Victim send Your Holy Spirit to my heart, my mind, my soul, my lips, and my hands, to every corner of my being so that I may celebrate, in the most dignified manner, these sacred mysteries of

I Daily Prayers and Devotions directed to God

Your Body and Your Blood of which You have made me a minister.

Clean my heart of all impurity, so that, having You as my only love, I may receive You as You deserve. Free my mind from every thought that could be contrary to what You have revealed to us in Your Word and through Your Church, I know that no matter how small it may be, it goes against the true faith, and without it, it is not possible to be open to Your mysteries.

Give me a holy fear of God to be able to perfectly understand that in a few moments I will be holding in my hands Your Most Holy Body in whose hands the heavens and the earth are held. Fill my whole being with Your Spirit and give death to the old man who dwells in me.

(*When celebrating it in public the following is also said*) Lord Jesus, grant me that with my gestures and my attitudes I may help Your holy people to discover more and more the deep meaning of the holy Mass, that is, the bloodless sacrifice offered for the salvation of the entire world. May I live this Holy Mass in such a way that acting in Your person, those who see me and hear me may be You who they see and hear.

May I celebrate this Holy Mass with the utmost respect and the spirit with which the Church, my mother, asks me to celebrate it. May the observance of each rubric be for me not an obstacle, but an expression of obedience without which it is impossible to please

You. Give me, also, Lord, the joy of knowing that in order to be one with me, You have become so close and small, and give me, O sacrificial Lamb, the same sentiments that accompanied You on the cross. Grant me, I humbly ask You, to experience the presence of Mary, my mother, with me at every moment of this holy Mass, the same maternal and loving presence that accompanied You at the foot of the cross.

In one word, Lord, help me - with the power of Your grace - to celebrate this Eucharist with the same fervor with which so many holy priests celebrated it throughout the centuries. That is, as if it were the first, the only and the last Mass of my existence in this world. Amen.

12. Prayer of the priest after the Holy Mass

Lord Jesus, friend, and companion in my journey, I thank You from the bottom of my heart for the privilege of having celebrated these sacred mysteries. You have chosen me, without any merit on my part, to use my voice and my hands in order to make Yourself present in the midst of Your holy people to instruct, feed, and sanctify them.

I trust that the way I have celebrated these sacred mysteries has been pleasing to You. Forgive

I Daily Prayers and Devotions directed to God

me if there was any distraction in my mind or if another thought for a moment occupied my heart. May the reverence, adoration, and admiration with which I sought to celebrate this holy Mass, have helped those who attended it to live and take more advantage of the fruits of Your salvation. I really hope that nothing of my personality, of my creation and of my spontaneity had been an obstacle for the power of the holy Mass had shone with its entire splendor.

I welcome You in my soul and in my heart; I fervently wish that upon entering in them You had not found any trace of sin or impurity. Lord, I am Your priest, I belong to You entirely. Do with me what You please and make of me a shepherd after Your own heart (cf. Jer 3:15). May I always sing with joy that *"the Lord is part of my inheritance and my cup, that You are the One who directs my destiny"* (Ps 16: 5).

Finally, help me to be faithful to my vocation, to persevere until the end of my life and that one day I may celebrate in Your company Your Paschal mysteries in the glory of Your heavenly Father. Amen.

13. Act of reparation

My loving Lord and my suffering Jesus, I am so sorry for all the offenses that You receive daily in the most holy Sacrament of the altar. I humbly beg Your forgiveness for those who neither believe in You, nor accept the holy doctrine about Your real presence. Moreover, I ask forgiveness for every sacrilegious act that, as a result of this lack of faith, is committed daily by bishops, priests, and laity against this most sacred Sacrament of love.

Accept my firm and my undoubtful confession that You are truly present in Body, Blood, Soul, and Divinity in each and every part of the holy host, and that every gesture of care, cleanliness and adoration falls always short in showing our love by receiving and contemplating this great heavenly gift.

Receive my unwavering hope in Your promises, founded on the belief that by living a life of sacrifice and obeying Your commandments, I will be able to one day enjoy eternal life with all Your angels and Your saints.

Lastly, I humbly ask You, O Lord, to receive my sincere love, a unique, exclusive and latreutic love to You alone, true God and true Man, the only way, truth and life, the only Name to which every knee must bend in the heavens, on the earth and in the abyss (cf. Phil 2: 10). Amen.

14. Prayer of abandonment

Lord and omnipotent God, You reward those who abandon themselves to You through faith in Your promises, I want, before Your divine majesty, before Saint Mary, my Mother, Saint Joseph, my father and lord, before all the

I Daily Prayers and Devotions directed to God

angels and in front of all the saints, solemnly declare my total, absolute and unconditional abandonment to Your divine will.

Through this act of abandonment, I accept all the crosses, illnesses, sacrifices, persecutions, humiliations, and insults to which Your divine will wants to subject me, whenever it is for Your greatest glory, for the sake of my brothers (my family) as well as for the salvation of my own soul. Amen.

(The following four prayers are to be said before and after the personal prayer, or mental prayer. The first two serve as an introduction and preparation for a time of silence and meditation and the last two as a conclusion. This meditation can be done in front of the Blessed Sacrament either exposed or in the tabernacle, but also such a prayer could be said anywhere the Lord is not present sacramentally).

15. Beginning mental prayer I

In the name of the Father, and of the Son and of the Holy Spirit. Amen. Good God assist me with Your grace so that this prayer that I will begin before You today may be pleasing to You, in the same way as it was the prayer of the tax collector who humbly visited Your holy temple (cf. Lk 18: 9-14). Let me enter into the depths of myself, only to find You and be with You, O God, in Whom lays the sole reason for my existence. Amen.

16. Beginning mental prayer II

In the name of the Father, and of the Son and of the Holy Spirit. Amen. My Lord and my God, at the beginning of this moment of personal prayer I humbly ask You to send Your Holy Spirit to enlighten my mind in the contemplation of Your mysteries, to silence my senses to be able to hear Your voice, to clean my heart so I can love You without limits, and to strengthen my will to obey You always without delay. Amen.

17. Ending mental prayer I

Sweet Lord and majestic King, I give You thanks for this time of prayer, for the truths that I have contemplated, for the paternal corrections You have made on me, for the sins You have forgiven me, for the inspired purposes and for the graces that in this moment of prayer You have bestowed on this, Your most humble and unworthy servant. Amen.

18. Ending mental prayer II

Lord Jesus, good teacher "... *"It is so good for us to be here"* (Mk 9: 5). I give You thanks for illuminating my mind and my heart with the light of Your grace. Forgive me if I have not heard Your voice calling me as I should. I renew my firm commitment to follow You wherever You go. May this time of prayer that You have allowed me to have may bear abundant fruits in pursuit of my salvation and the salvation of the entire world. Amen.

19. Prayer to God the Father

Father in heaven, *"... before the mountains were begotten, and the earth and the world were born, from eternity to eternity, You are God"* (Ps 90: 2). It was then, in eternity, that You begat Your beloved Son, the Eternal Word, for Whom and by Whom, working also with the Holy Spirit, together - as if they were Your two hands (cf. St. Irenaeus of Lyon) - You created everything that exists. I praise You and thank You for the greatness of Your work of creation superseded only by Your wondrous work of redemption which opened the doors of salvation to me and to the entire world.

When the fullness of time came, You sent Your beloved Son so that through Him we could know Your face, so that whoever sees Him could see You in Him, O Good Father (cf. Jn 14: 9). By becoming a man and sharing in our own human nature, He made possible for us to be truly -in Him- Your children and call You Father. In this way, You became for us not only a creator and sovereign God, but also a God so close to us who invoke Your protection and Your providence as Your children.

Finally, to fulfill Your will, from the altar of the cross, in order to save us from sin and death, Your Son offered Himself to You in sacrifice (cf. Ga 4:4). It is in every celebration of the Holy Mass that, as member of the Body of Your Son, which is the Church, I offer - represented by Your priest- the Body and Blood of Your beloved Son in holy sacrifice for my own salvation and for the salvation of the whole world.

From You, Good Father, all paternity proceeds in heaven and on earth (cf. Eph 3:15) and that is why I solemnly declare that I want to direct all my life and my existence in humble service to Your divine majesty. Today I want to recognize and proclaim before the whole world Your sovereignty, Your power and Your authority, which are above any power either in heaven or on earth and even in the abyss.

With filial trust I place my whole life into Your hands as a loving Father and I offer to You the totality of my being, of my will, of my freedom and of everything that I am and that I possess. Everything is Yours, Good and Holy Father, take it.

Let everything I do be oriented to praise You and to give You glory always in the person of Your beloved Son Whom You have asked us to listen to (cf. Mt 17: 5). Use me as You see fit so that every man and every woman know that, believing in Your beloved Son, they can also become Your daughters and Your sons and enjoy in Your copious benefits as well in this life as in Your glory in heaven.

That through my words and actions, through my example and testimony, in a way that leave no doubt, may I always proclaim that only through Jesus, Your beloved Son and my dear Lord, and through nobody else, it is found the only access to You, O great Father of mercies. Never forsake me and grant me that one day, following

I Daily Prayers and Devotions directed to God

the teachings of Your Son, may I deserve to dwell forever in Your heavenly house. I ask all this in the name of Your Son, Jesus Christ, for Whom I have full confidence that You will listen to my prayer (cf. Jn 16: 24). Amen.

20. Prayer of Divine Mercy

God of Infinite and Divine Mercy who offers Your heart to those in misery and distributes Your gifts among those who do not deserve it, we adore You, we praise You, and for Your infinite mercy we thank You.

With great mercy You created man and instead of treating him as a simple creature - although You made him the most perfect creature over the face of the earth (cf. Ps 8:5) -You planted in him the seed of divine sonship, thus raising him above the angels. *Our Father and Glory be....*

God of love, we thank You for Your infinite mercy.

But, even after giving man the gift of Your presence and friendship, he preferred darkness and sin, and although he disobeyed Your commands, *"You did not abandon him to the power of death, but helped all men to seek and find You" (Eucharistic Prayer IV, Roman Missal).* Our Father and Glory be....

God of love, we thank You for Your infinite mercy.

By Your mercy, You led humanity through a long history of salvation and even though You sent them prophets and shepherds with the message of Your Word, human beings kept rejecting You over and over again. *Our father ...and Glory be....*

God of love, we thank You for Your infinite mercy.

When the fullness of time came and after receiving only ungratefulness and rejection from men, Your mercy sent Your beloved Son, Jesus Christ, through Whom You showed Your love and Your solicitude in an extreme way. Men, however, preferred not to listen to Him, rejecting Him and hanging Him on a tree. *Our Father and Glory be....*

God of love, we thank You for Your infinite mercy.

Your mercy, however, was shed even more copiously when You raised Him from the dead, opening the doors of heaven to all who accept, in the name of Christ, the only salvation that comes from You. *Our father and Glory be....*

God of love, we thank You for Your infinite mercy.

This same mercy is offered in the holy Church where You, Good God, constantly welcome all repentant sinners by placing this same salvation within their reach. *Our Father and Glory be....*

I Daily Prayers and Devotions directed to God

God of love, we thank You for Your infinite mercy.

Let us pray.

For all these benefits, Lord, we thank You and ask You not to get weary of forgiving us, so that thankful for Your countless benefits, we may one day, by Your infinite mercy, be received into Your glory in order to contemplate forever the beauty of Your face through Your Son Jesus Christ, through Whom Your divine mercy has been copiously poured out upon the world. Amen.

21. Prayer of liberation against idolatry and superstition

Lord God, the only and true Creator and Savior of all that exists, it is my firm will to solemnly and publicly confess before Your divine Majesty, before Mary, my Mother and my father, Saint Joseph, before all the angels and saints of heaven and before every living being that dwells in this world, that I place all my love, my faith and my hope only and exclusively in You.

I renounce, therefore, every kind of superstition, which is to attribute some kind of supernatural power to things, people, actions or events that do not have it. I know that all this comes from the devil, the enemy of the human race who, using all kinds of lies and deceptions when presenting these works of death, seeks only my destruction (cf. 1 Pt 5: 8; Jn 8: 44; Rev 12: 9).

I promise, from this moment on, that I will never have anything to do for any reason, for any motive and under any circumstance, with any kind of seer, witch, sorcerer, fortune teller, card reader, or any kind of shaman or guru (cf. 2 R 21: 6; Is 2: 6; 65: 11-12); I will not guide my life by any horoscope, nor will I seek to know the future in any form or method, even if the end is presented as good (cf. Dt 4: 19; 18: 10-11). I also refuse to partake in any kind of syncretism, which is to mix different beliefs with the unique beauty of the Catholic faith. I know that all this seriously offends You and puts my eternal salvation at risk.

I promise and solemnly swear that I will prefer death before vowing or prostrating myself before an idol or before anything that is not You, the only and Almighty God. Only in You, Holy among all saints, lies my true peace, my harmony and my bodily and spiritual balance, and that is why I also promise that I will refrain from practicing all kinds of meditation or body movements - such as yoga, reiki, taichí or practices of that kind - that have their origin in a spirituality, a philosophy or a notion about You, different from that which You have revealed to me in Your Word and taught through the holy Catholic Church, my mother (cf. Ex 3: 5; Rom 1: 25).

Omnipotent Lord, I promise that I will never put my life, my present or my future in anything or anyone that is not You, God of blessings; and I declare that, only in accordance with Your divine and loving will, will I forever guide my whole life (cf. Acts 18:15; Rev 21:19).

I Daily Prayers and Devotions directed to God

I infinitely thank You because of all these practices of darkness that come from the ignorance of sin and death, You, Good Lord, have delivered me through the knowledge of Your Gospel (cf. 1 Pt 2: 9). I beg You with profound humility for the grace to carry out, faithfully and for the rest of my life, this promise that I solemnly make to You today.

Mary, my Mother, Saint Joseph, provident father, Saint Michael, the Archangel, my guardian angel protect me from the insidious attacks of the enemy and do not allow me to separate myself from the truth of the Gospel which is alone where true freedom can be found (cf. Jn 8: 32). Amen.

22. Prayer for the poor souls in purgatory

Lord and God of justice, sovereign king of life and death, I beg You to receive my humble prayer for all the poor souls who left this world free of their sins, but still in need of purification.

Your mercy is so great that not only have You given us in this life the forgiveness of sins, but, in the event that death would surprise us having in our souls the wounds produced by our disobedience, we could be purified outside of this world in a place of suffering and penance to achieve the perfection and holiness necessary to enter Your glory.

There, these souls can no longer deserve, nor do anything for themselves, but, patiently, and formed in humility, await the help of our prayers and the power of the sacrifice of the holy Mass in which they place all of their hope.

Help these poor souls, Lord, who have been redeemed by Your Blood, who by Your grace find themselves already free from eternal damnation, that they may soon, after the time of their purification, meet with Your saints in Your kingdom. I ask You especially for ... *(Mention the deceased person for whom you wish to pray)*.

Good Lord do not let us -who still remain in this world- forget these poor souls who are in such great need of our help. May many sacrifices and rosaries be offered for their benefit; may the cemeteries be visited with faith and many prayers elevated over their graves. Help us to have the necessary disposition to gain indulgences on their behalf. But above all, Lord, may there always be a holy Mass celebrated on their benefit.

May they one day, already crowned with Your glory, receive us grateful at the gates of Your eternal kingdom where You live and reign in the unity of the Holy Spirit forever and ever. Amen.

23. Prayer of a family at the Nativity scene on Christmas

O Father Most holy, on this holy night in which Your angels proclaimed with joy: *"Glory to God in the highest and on earth peace to people of good will"* (Lk 2:14) this family wants to thank You for the priceless gift of Your Son. This Son

I Daily Prayers and Devotions directed to God

of Yours, made a small and helpless child, we have worshiped and placed with deep reverence in this manger prepared with our own hands in the heart of our home. With this gesture we want to express that Your Son, for Whom there was no place in the inn (cf. v. 7), is always welcome in this humble house where we proclaim Him as our King and our Lord.

This night in which we remember the birth of Your Son, may all the members of this family be filled with love for the many benefits and blessings You have bestowed upon us. May we be worthy to welcome into our homes the peace that this Child has brought to the whole world. Do not ever let us use our freedom to leave Your holy company, since through Your beloved Son You have come so close to us with the only purpose of giving fulfillment to our lives.

By contemplating the images of Mary and Joseph, filled with joy, with their eyes fixed on the baby Jesus laid in the manger, may we imitate their virtues and their obedience in the faithful fulfillment of Your will. By beholding the poverty of this manger, may we always know that true happiness cannot be found in money, nor in possessions, but only in having Your Son as a guest of our souls.

Do not allow, Lord, that any of the members of this family stray from Your path. You know our hearts; they are poor and weak. May Jesus always find a manger in our hearts so He can be born in them. And if any of us, at any point of our lives, confused by the lies of this world which did not receive Your Son (cf. Jn 1:11, 14:17), had the misfortune of departing from You, as You did with the lost sheep, come in search of us and bring us back to Your flock where only true happiness can be found -the same happiness that Your Son has brought us with His birth on this night of peace and love-. May the whole world believe in You and accept the redemption that, in this little Child, You have made available to everyone. Amen.

24. Prayer at the beginning of a pilgrimage to holy Land

Lord Jesus, *"my heart is glad and my tongue rejoices"* (Ps 16:9) because in Your goodness You have granted me the grace to begin this pilgrimage through those holy places where You were born, lived, died, and rose from the dead for me and for the whole world. How can I not thank You for this gesture of love and predilection towards me?

My feet will step now on the land which You promised Abraham as an inheritance (cf. Gen 12: 1-3), the land where Moses led Your people through the desert in the midst of great wonders and miracles (cf. Ex 1: 1 -27) and in which, after a long pilgrimage, Your people entered guided by Joshua (cf. Jos 4: 1-13). It was on this earth that both David and Solomon were kings, whose lives were pleasing to You (cf. 2 Sam 5: 1-5). Thus, through the prophets and throughout the centuries, Your promises of salvation resonated in every corner of this land (cf. Heb 1:1).

I Daily Prayers and Devotions directed to God

And when the fullness of time came, it was on this blessed land that You became a man, lived among us (cf. Jn 1:14) and entered our history. Your feet stepped on this earth and in this very land the proclamation of the good news was heard for the first time (cf. Mc 1: 5). This holy ground also witnessed Your power, which You showed through great signs, miracles and healings (cf. Mt 8: 14-17; Mk 1: 21-34; Lk 4: 31-41). It was this sacred land that shook when it saw You driving out demons and raising the dead (cf. Mk 5: 13; Lk 8: 40-57. 7: 11-17; Jn 11: 17-44).

And when Your hour came, it was also this land that opened itself reverently to receive Your precious Blood, which You shed during Your Passion in which You suffered unspeakable mistreatments until giving up Your own life on the tree of the cross planted in this same land (cf. Lk 23: 26-56). In the womb of this very land, You rested for three days, and then - on this very ground - the glory of Your resurrection shone (cf. Jn 20: 3-18). And finally, it was from here that You ascended into the heavens to sit at the right hand of Your heavenly Father, to reign as victorious King over the entire universe (cf. Acts 1: 9-11).

From this sacred land, Lord of infinite glory, Your Apostles went out to the ends of the earth, carrying in their hearts, lit by the Spirit, the fire of Your message of salvation (cf. Mk 16: 15-20). And thanks to them, from these very ends of the earth came to my ears the news of Your redemption. Now I have returned here where it all began, to strengthen my faith as Your witness and return home exclaiming with joy: *"That which was from the beginning, which we have heard, which we have seen with our eyes, which we have looked at and our hands have touched concerning the Word of life we also proclaim to you"* (1 Jn 1: 3).

From the bottom of my heart, I thank You, Lord, thank You so much for allowing me to be here. While I am here, let me live again what You lived in this land, so that I may love You more and proclaim Your name with every breath of my being. I believe, Lord, I do believe! At the beginning of this pilgrimage, I beg You to walk with me as You did with the disciples of Emmaus, open my heart with Your Word (cf. Lk 24: 13-35), and grant me, Lord, that one day, taken by Your hand, I may enter into the promised land of Your kingdom, where You will make me a partaker of the ineffable glory of Your presence. Amen.

25. Prayer to Christ in His Passion

Lord Jesus, innocent Lamb, burdened in the garden for my many sins,
- I contemplate You with deep devotion, who cried on the rock for my many iniquities. *Our Father, Hail Mary and Glory be....*

By Your cross and Your Passion, have mercy on me.

Lord Jesus, innocent Lamb, humiliated in prison for my many sins,
- I contemplate You with deep devotion, bound and mistreated by my many miseries. *Our Father, Hail Mary and Glory be....*
By Your cross and Your Passion, have mercy on me.

I Daily Prayers and Devotions directed to God

Lord Jesus, innocent Lamb, cruelly scourged for my many sins,
> - I contemplate You with deep devotion, mocked and spurned by my many faults. *Our Father, Hail Mary and Glory be....*
> *By Your cross and Your Passion, have mercy on me.*

Lord Jesus, innocent Lamb, cruelly crowned with thorns for my many sins,
> - I contemplate You with deep devotion, tortured and ridiculed by my countless ingratitudes. *Our Father, Hail Mary and Glory be....*

> *By Your cross and Your Passion, have mercy on me.*

Lord Jesus, innocent Lamb and suffering servant under the terrible weight of the cross of my many sins,
> - I contemplate You with deep devotion, overwhelmed and afflicted under the burden of my repeated disobediences. *Our Father, Hail Mary and Glory be....*

> *By Your cross and Your Passion, have mercy on me.*

Lord Jesus, innocent Lamb, crucified and murdered by my many sins,
> - I contemplate You with deep devotion, and I adore You, hanging from the cross because of my many abominations. *Our Father, Hail Mary and Glory be....*
> *By Your cross and Your Passion, have mercy on me.*

Prayers of the Soul

Let us pray.

Lord Jesus, suffering servant, You came down from heaven to participate in the drama of human life and carry on Your shoulders my sins and the sins of the whole world. I beg You to have mercy on me, a poor and miserable sinner. Grant me that by meditating on Your holy Passion, my heart may be filled with love for You, so that by serving and pleasing You in this life, I may deserve, after a holy death, the eternal life that You have earned for me through Your sufferings. I ask this of You Who loved me and gave Yourself for me (cf. Gal 2: 21) and Who lives and reigns forever and ever. Amen.

26. Prayer to Christ in His Most Precious Blood

Lord Jesus, Most loving King, I prostrate myself and adore with deep reverence the glory of Your most pure and most holy Blood that, upon being spilled on this earth, caused the redemption of the entire world.

For all occasions, during Your Sacred Passion, in which Your Holy Body shed Your Precious Blood, I implore You to have mercy on me, a sinner, and on the entire world.

For the anguish that made You sweat Blood which — like drops of dew - began a deluge of universal grace. *Our Father, Hail Mary and Glory be....*

I Daily Prayers and Devotions directed to God

O most Pure and Holy Blood wash me.

For the slaps and blows You received during Your arrest and that caused Your beautiful face to be covered with Your redeeming Blood as a sacred anointing of eternal life. *Our Father, Hail Mary and Glory be....*

O most Pure and Holy Blood wash me.

For the many scourges inflicted on Your holy back which without compassion was tortured and torn apart, causing to flow from them rivers of redemption. *Our Father, Hail Mary and Glory be....*
O most Pure and Holy Blood, wash me.

For the crown of thorns which was brutally imposed on You opening in Your holy head extremely painful wounds which released a torrent of infinite grace. *Our Father, Hail Mary and Glory be....*

O most Pure and Holy Blood, wash me.

For Your right shoulder where Your saving cross rested, opening in it such a huge wound, the most painful of all, from which an endless source of mercy sprang. *Our Father, Hail Mary and Glory be....*
O most Pure and Holy Blood wash me.

For the wounds that were reopened when Your holy robes were torn from Your Body, ripping Your divine flesh and letting Your precious Blood run once more into streams of salvation. *Our Father, Hail Mary and Glory be....*

O most Pure and Holy Blood wash me.

For the merciless nails which pierced Your holy hands and feet, giving way to an infinite ocean of sanctification. *Our Father, Hail Mary and Glory be....*

O most Pure and Holy Blood wash me.

For the cruel lance which pierced Your side bringing a sudden flow of Blood and Water from Your loving heart emptying thus Your Holy Body of the last drop of infinite love. *Our Father, Hail Mary and Glory be....*

O most Pure and Holy Blood wash me.

Let us pray.

By Your precious Blood shed for all my sins and for the sins of the entire world, Lord, have mercy on me and on all sinners. May Your ministers, Lord, who in each Eucharist distribute Your Glorious Blood, do so with extreme care, respect and adoration, since by virtue of this same Precious Blood, those of us who were dead have returned to life. Amen.

I Daily Prayers and Devotions directed to God

27. Prayer to the Holy Spirit I

Holy Spirit of God the Father and of God the Son, Lord and Giver of life, Sanctifier of mankind, descend into my soul and cleanse me completely, enter my mind that I may understand Your motions, give light to my eyes that I may see what is right, purify my mouth to proclaim Your Word, recreate my hands so that they become Your instruments, change my heart into one capable of loving You without measure, guide my steps so that I may always walk in Your presence and take my will so it may become one with Yours.

In one word, Lord, enter my spirit and make it fruitful, strong, and docile to Your inspirations so that what I cannot do because of my weakness, You can do through me. Make me thus a faithful instrument of Your fruitful action in the world. Amen.

28. Prayer to the Holy Spirit II

Holy Spirit, give me wisdom to understand what God the Father and the Son want from me. Give me understanding to scrutinize Your Word. Give me counsel to always do the right thing. Give me fortitude so I may never succumb to the power of the evil one. Give me knowledge to distinguish the essential from the secondary. Give me piety to deal with God as He deserves. And give me fear of God to never forget to Whom I must answer at the end of my life.

Wherever I go, Spirit of God, help me to take Your love in the midst of a world of hate; let me radiate the joy of knowing that only You alone are enough, make me communicate the peace that consists in having You within; that I may be patient with the defects of others; filled with longanimity in times of crisis; that I may be kind, always willing to give more; good with those who need it most; meek, slow to anger and rich in mercy; faithful to Your Word and to the faith of the Church; modest, never vain, or superficial; continent, always restraining my passions; and chaste, living not according to my flesh, but according to Your inspirations. Amen.

29. Spiritual Communion I

Jesus, beloved Lord and God, on my knees in front of Your sublime presence, I thank You for coming down from heaven and staying among us; in doing so once again You renew Your redemptive sacrifice, generously offered for my salvation and for the salvation of the entire world. Nothing in this world would fill me with more joy than being able to receive You sacramentally in my soul, but for now this is not possible.

For this, I humbly ask for Your forgiveness and I beg You, most sweet Jesus, that soon my soul may be able to receive You worthily. Grant me this grace; so that, by becoming one with You, I may deserve that all Your promises be fulfilled in me. I adore You, Lord, and I confess You as my God and my Savior, truly present in this most Holy Sacrament of the altar. Amen.

30. Spiritual Communion II

What does a soul that dares to receive You in Holy Communion have to resemble? It must have the purity of Your Mother's womb, the holiness of the hearts of the saints, the beauty of the temple of Jerusalem, the transparency of the waters that descend from the mountains and the whiteness of the snow. In short, Lord, all that on my own merit, my poor soul is incapable of resembling.

For that reason, I cannot receive You now, but I humbly ask You to come to me, at least spiritually, so that my spirit craves You more and more and soon, after reconciling with You and being transformed by Your grace, I may receive You as You deserve in my poor heart, O admirable Sacrament of love. Amen.

31. Spiritual Communion III

Lord Jesus, adored by the angels, proclaimed by the apostles, witnessed by the martyrs, imitated by the virgins and faithfully followed by all the saints, I, humbly, ask You to prepare my heart that I may receive You with the same fervor, the same devotion and the same faith with which all these great men and women received You in this great Sacrament of the altar. Amen.

32. Visit to the Blessed Sacrament I

Lord Jesus Blessed God, loving prisoner of men, here I am prostrated before Your most high majesty, God of heaven and earth, incarnate Word, Son of the Father and Mary; true, real and substantially present in this most sublime Sacrament of the altar.

I adore You as my God and my Lord, and I beg You to never permit me to forget the greatness of this amazing mystery that brings us Your presence in our midst. Help me that before You, in this moment of prayer, my heart may be filled with love, my mind be illuminated with Your truths and my will be strengthened to faithfully follow Your commands. Blessed and Holy God, King of ineffable love, Eucharistic Jesus, I pledge to adore You with all my being and for all the days of my life. Amen.

33. Visit to the Blessed Sacrament II

Lord Jesus, Eucharistic God, I confess with my mind, with my will and with my heart, that You are truly and substantially present in this most holy Sacrament of the altar in the same way as You are sitting on the right hand of God the Father.

My whole being worships You prostrated before Your infinite majesty, and I beg You to cleanse my heart and my soul in such a way that I could receive You with dignity in the Holy Mass, and thus, enjoy some day the fulfillment of Your divine promises. Amen.

34. Visit to the Blessed Sacrament III

Eucharistic Lord Jesus, living bread that came down from heaven, blessed and sacrosanct is Your presence in our midst, prisoner for love in all the tabernacles throughout the whole world in order to be loved and worshiped. Make me, Lord, to seek You in deep and true prayer, and in seeking You make me know You fully, and in knowing You like this, grant me the gift of loving You with every fiber of my being. O Eucharistic God, may You be now and forever blessed and worshiped by each heart and in each soul in every corner of the whole world. Amen.

35. Visit to the Blessed Sacrament IV

Jesus, Good Shepherd, living bread that has come down from heaven, whoever eats Your Body and drinks Your Blood will never die (cf. Jn 6:54). In this Sacrament of love in which You have wanted to remain substantially present, You show us, to those who have been redeemed with Your cross, Your love and Your fatherly solicitude.

Help me to always adore You as my God and my Lord, and to prepare myself inwardly by resisting the wickedness of the evil one, so that, conserving Your grace, I may receive You with dignity in each

Eucharist and thus, always remain in communion with You. Amen.

36. Visit to the Blessed Sacrament V

Jesus, Son of the living God, I confess with all my heart, my mind and my will that You are truly present in this admirable Sacrament of the Eucharist. I faithfully profess the perennial faith of Your Church, my mother, who has confessed and taught Your real presence in this Sacrament since You instituted it on the night of Your Passion in the Cenacle (cf. Lk 22: 19-20).

I faithfully and undoubtedly confess everything that Your Church has deepened and taught about this mystery throughout the centuries, through the holy fathers and the councils. I humbly beseech You to strengthen my faith so that my inner disposition, as well as my external behavior, both in worshiping and in receiving You, be that of respect, admiration and deep gratitude for Your loving abasement in the humility of this holy Host. Amen.

37. Litany of a Sinner

Lord, have mercy on me. **Lord, have mercy on me.**
Christ, have mercy on me. **Christ, have mercy on me.**
Lord, have mercy on me. **Lord, have mercy on me.**
Christ, hear me. **Christ, graciously hear me.**
Lord, salvation of my soul.
     Have mercy on me.
Lord, sweet Redeemer...

I Daily Prayers and Devotions directed to God

Lord, Whom I have mocked without limits, ...
Lord, against Whom I have blasphemed, ...
Lord, Whom I have offended so much, ...
Lord, crucified by my sins...
Lord, Whose mercy is higher than the heavens, ...
Lord, Whose clemency exceeds the depths of the sea, ...
Lord, overwhelmed by my evil works, ...
Lord, Whom I have spit in the face, ...
Lord, scourged by my disordered passions, ...
Lord, crowned with my infidelities, ...
Lord, humiliated by my ingratitude, ...
Lord, pierced by my miseries, ...
Lord, murdered by my iniquity, ...
Lord, buried by my indifference and by my indolence, ...

O Jesus, do not abandon me to the consequences of my sins. **_Rescue me, Lord._**
O Jesus, do not leave me alone, ...
O Jesus, look at my nothingness, ...
O Jesus, look at my emptiness, ...
O Jesus, look at my anguish, ...
O Jesus, look at my unworthiness, ...
O Jesus, look at my miseries, ...
O Jesus, look at my dejection, ...
O Jesus, look at my poor soul, ...
O Jesus, look at my broken spirit, ...

Good Shepherd, guide me always.
Heal me my God.
Good Shepherd, wash me whole, ...
Good Shepherd, heal me soul and body, ...
Good Shepherd, restore me from within, ...
Good Shepherd, recreate me as in the beginning, ...
Good Shepherd, that I may see, ...

Prayers of the Soul

Good Shepherd, that I may listen, ...
Good Shepherd, that I may walk, ...
Good Shepherd, that I may have life in abundance,...
Good Shepherd, that I may love You, ...
Good Shepherd, that I may prefer death rather than sin, ...
Good Shepherd, that I may survive Your judgment, ...
Good Shepherd, help me to repair the damage I have done, ...
Good Shepherd, do not let me depart from You, ...
Good Shepherd, purify and wash clean my body from all impurity, ...
Good Shepherd, give me back what I have lost, ...
Good Shepherd, I am naked, ...
Good Shepherd, I am afraid, ...
Good Shepherd, give me to drink, ...
Good Shepherd, feed me, ...
Good Shepherd, let me recognize Your voice, ...

For having turned away from Your love,
Listen to me and forgive me, Lord.
For leaving Your loving and paternal house, ...
For wishing You didn't exist, ...
For despising Your gifts, ...
For using them to offend You, ...
For thinking only of me, ...
For using others for my pleasure, ...
For choosing the world instead of You, ...
For not loving You, ...
For my sadness, ...
For my bitterness, ...
For my many betrayals, ...
For my many ingratitudes, ...

I Daily Prayers and Devotions directed to God

For my countless evils, ...
For serving the devil, ...
For letting myself be seduced by him, ...
For seducing others in his name, ...
For my impenitence, ...
For my imprudence, ...
For all my sins, ...

Jesus, faithful Shepherd,
> **Do not let me get lost.**

Jesus, eternal Priest,
> **Intercede before the Father for me.**

Jesus, innocent Victim,
> **Forgive me for putting You to death.**

Jesus, Gate of the kingdom,
> **Do not let me out.**

Jesus, only Way,
> **Guide my steps.**

Jesus, absolute Truth,
> **I believe in You.**

Jesus, fullness of Life,
> **May I never lose You.**

Jesus, firm Rock,
> **May I build my life on You.**

Jesus, Prince of peace,
> **Fill with it my soul.**

Jesus, long awaited Messiah,
> **May I always receive You with joy.**

May Your grace act on me,
> **And may I never leave You again.**

Mary Immaculate, refuge of sinners,
> **Show me the way of salvation.**
> **Let us pray.**

O Lord, Good and Merciful Father, turn Your compassionate countenance toward this poor and miserable sinner who comes to You contrite and humiliated by his many offenses; transform me from within, change my stony heart into one made of flesh and make me love You with every fiber of my being. Grant me, Gracious and Kind God, that I may prefer death before offending You again, thus moving away from You, who are the source of all my life and my happiness. Separated from You, Holy and Eternal God, there is only darkness and misfortune. Accept, therefore, my humble prayer, not because of my merits, for I have none, but through the merits of Your beloved Son who loved me and gave Himself to death for me (cf. Ga 2: 20). Amen.

II PRAYERS TO THE VIRGIN MARY, ANGELS AND SAINTS

National Gallery of Art, Washington, D.C. Small
Cowper Madonna, Italian Renaissance painting, oil
on panel by Raphael (1483-1520).

II Prayers to the Virgin Mary, Angels and Saints

38. Act of consecration to Our Lady

Dear Blessed Mother, most Holy Virgin Mary, accept the offering of my life, of all that I am and all that I possess, my thoughts, my dreams and my loves. I put everything at your feet, dispose of me as you please.

I solemnly and publicly declare myself to be not only your son (daughter), but your soldier, ready for battle, beginning with myself and against everything that opposes the will of Jesus, my God and my Lord. Grant me the necessary graces that I need of which, the Lord has wanted you to be His incomparable mediatrix. Prepare my soul so that more and more like yours, I may present it perfect, holy and beyond reproach on the day I am called before the majesty of your beloved Son. Amen.

39. Prayer to Our Lady of Mount Carmel

O Blessed Mary, Queen and Empress of the Holy Mountain, turn your ear toward me, Your most humble son (daughter), with great mercy and compassion, protect me under your maternal mantle from the forces of darkness that seek the damnation of my soul.

Grant me the gift of prayer and contemplation to ponder all the fundamental truths concerning human life and Christian faith so that I may always live in holiness.

And when the moment of my death comes, if it were necessary to go to purgatory, by the grace conferred through your holy scapular, rescue me soon from its flames and once purified from every imperfection and attachment, take me in your bosom to the kingdom of your Son and my Lord. Amen.

40. Prayer to the Most Holy Mother of God

Mary, Mother of the true God, the Heart of Jesus was formed in your womb; in that way you became a tent of encounter between God and men. Look, then, with pity on this son (daughter) of yours whom your beloved Son rescued from darkness into His admirable light (cf. 1 Pt 2: 9).

Have compassion on me, pure Mother; do not let go of my hand, cover my smallness with your maternal mantle and obtain for me the graces of which God has wanted to make you a privileged dispenser.

Give me an unwavering love and devotion to your Immaculate Heart. Grant me to be constant in the recitation of the Holy Rosary, a powerful weapon against evil. Teach me to be chaste and pure like your Son. Help me to recognize Him today in the

II Prayers to the Virgin Mary, Angels and Saints

unfathomable mystery of the Eucharist, as well as among the poorest and neediest.

Mary, living Gospel, nobody knows Jesus better than you. Help me also to know Him and love Him with all my strength. By the blessed power of your intercession, protect me from any temptation and make me like you, so I too may crush the head of the ancient serpent.

Mother of goodness, accept the offering I make before you today of my whole life, of everything I am and everything I have, and grant me to live with the same conviction that you lived all your life, so that also in me God's will may always be done (cf. Lk 1:38). Amen.

41. Prayer to Mary Most Holy Mother of God in her dogmas

Holy Mary in whom God has done great wonders (cf. Lk 1:49), turn your beautiful and pure face towards us and accept our humble praise.

You entered this world like the dawn: clean, holy and spotless. In this way you defeated the evil snake that had subjugated the entire human race.

Hail Mary, full of grace...

Prayers of the Soul

Mary Immaculate, you who are free from the reach of the evil one, those who pilgrim in this world implore your protection.

The Word of God, in order to become incarnate, entered into your womb as light passes through a glass, without breaking it, or staining it (cf. St. Pius X). That is how your virginity was preserved, before, during and after childbirth.

Hail Mary, full of grace…

Mary, Virgin most pure, in you, God worked a great portent of greatness; we who pilgrim in this world implore your protection.

In a unique act of infinite grace, you gave birth to the one who brought you into existence. So, He who created the heavens and the earth and all that they contain was pleased to make you His Mother.

Hail Mary, full of grace…

Mary, Mother of God, to you who gave birth to the Son of God, we who pilgrim in this world implore your protection.

It was not possible that the sacrosanct sanctuary of your body that carried the Eternal Word could suffer the corruption of death. Thus, when the course of your earthly life was completed, you were carried in body and soul to the heavens by the hands of the angels.

II Prayers to the Virgin Mary, Angels and Saints

Hail Mary, full of grace…

Mary, assumed to the heavens, great is the glory that God has given you; we who pilgrimage in this world implore your protection.

Let us pray

O God, who has crowned Mary with great wonders in the time of our salvation, inspire ever more those of us who live in this world to recognize and praise these great Marian mysteries, so we may please You and proclaim with joy Your saving work in the world. Through Christ, Our Lord. Amen.

42. Prayer to the Immaculate Heart of Mary

Mother most pure, at the time of your conception, God modeled your heart, knowing that you would be the Mother of His Son. That is why he made it holy and pure, worthy of loving without any trace of sin the One Who in turn would love the world to the point of giving up His own life.

Immaculate Heart of Mary, pray for us.

It was your noble Heart, Blessed Mother, which, even before your womb, received the Savior of the world. That is why when the Word descended into your bosom, it was not a strange place where He came, but to its temple in whose heart He already had His dwelling place.

Immaculate Heart of Mary, pray for us.

And He who modeled your Heart, from your Heart then took the nobility and goodness to form His. And hence, the Word became man and in your womb, the sun of justice grew under the warm love of your immaculate Heart.

Immaculate Heart of Mary, pray for us.
How sublime was the mystery of communion between your Immaculate Heart with that of the Child Jesus. Such a union reflected not only the love of mother and son, but that of God and creature, infinite love entwining two hearts. As His Mother, you educated His, while He, as God, gave life and sustenance to yours.

Immaculate Heart of Mary, pray for us.

The most noble and tender of hearts was pierced by the sword - as prophesied by Simeon (cf. Lk 2:35) - suffering the torture of seeing the heart of her Son pierced by the soldier's spear. Therefore, Holy Mother, you are rightly acclaimed as a co-redemptrix, because what Jesus suffered in His heart during His Passion, you suffered in yours for the salvation of the entire world.

Immaculate Heart of Mary, pray for us.
On the glorious morning of the Resurrection, there was no other heart that was filled with more joy by seeing the Risen One than yours, O Queen of heaven. We ask you, with deep humility, that we may always rejoice in the certainty that in your Sacred Heart and in that of your

II Prayers to the Virgin Mary, Angels and Saints

beloved Son, we will find our safest and unshakable refuge.

Immaculate Heart of Mary, pray for us.
Let us pray

Eternal and Merciful God, Who fashioned the Immaculate Heart of the Mother of Your Son and filled it with love and tenderness, we humbly beg You to fill our hearts with Your grace, so that, cleansed of all impurity, we may please You in the same way You were pleased with the holiness of the Virgin Mary to whose Immaculate Heart we consecrate ourselves and our families today. All of this we ask of You Who live and reign forever and ever. Amen.

43. Prayer to the Virgin Mary in times of distress

O Glorious Virgin Mary, under your powerful mantle, give me refuge as I go through these difficult and dark times. You crushed the snake's head and thanks to the divine power, the devil could never touch you. Free me, then, from his insidious attacks. Protect me, O powerful Mother, at this hour of distress and do not let me succumb to adversity. Let it not be said that those who implored your protection were disappointed.

Listen to me as your son (daughter), you who are the best of mothers. Never take your immaculate presence away from me. May I have your courage, the same courage that kept you standing at the side of the cross of your beloved Son (cf. Jn 19:25).

Finally, good and kind Mother, do not let me lose hope but on the contrary, give me the certainty of knowing that after this storm and this darkness, calm and light will come, and with them a new dawn where I will thank you for all the favors you will bestow on this your most humble servant. May you always be blessed, O Mary, Mother Most beloved! Amen.

44. Prayer to our Sorrowful Mother

Most sorrowful Mother, much deeper than all the waters of the oceans are the pains and sufferings torturing your Immaculate Heart. How profound is your loneliness and how inexpressible your agony, O suffering Mother! Surely the prophetic words you heard from Simeon when he saw you in the temple when presenting the baby Jesus come now to your mind: *"and behold, a sword will pierce your heart"* (cf. Lk 2:35). Your many pains come from gazing on the lifeless Body of your Son and behold, your Son is dead because of my many sins and transgressions.

Here then, O sorrowful Mother, I prostrate myself with profound humility and shame before you. Forgive me, I implore you, O good Mother, and let my prayers, my repentance and my penances be the fibers that weave the finest handkerchief worthy of wiping away your copious tears and thus, help to mitigate a little the suffering of your loving Heart.

Let me now accompany you and watch with you the glorious Body of your Redeemer and mine. Let me look at His holy wounds and in them recognize the high price that He paid for my many miseries and transgressions. I firmly promise you not to sin anymore, to dedicate my life to the service of your Son's Gospel and with my love and devotion for you, provide some comfort to your afflicted and tortured Heart, O sorrowful Mother of my God and Savior. Amen.

45. Prayer to Saint Michael the Archangel

Saint Michael the Archangel, powerful general of the heavenly hosts, your power and your courage have no equal among the hosts of heavens. You who, in order to defend the honor of the Most High, bravely fought against the devil, that rebellious angel, who, being the most beautiful and luminous of all spiritual beings, chose, consumed with pride, to rise against the One who had brought him into existence. You and your army of holy angels won in great battle under the maxim: *"Who is like God?"* and clothed with the power of the Most High, with divine justice, threw the devil and his minions into hell to be punished forever without any hope (cf. Is 14: 12).

Come to my defense at this difficult hour in which the forces of evil return with great fury to desolate the earth with their lies and deceptions. Come to my aid, O great general of the kingdom of God; defend me with your sword of divine and inextinguishable fire against the destructive and insidious fire of the devil. Free me from his seductions and defeat him as you did on that glorious day.

Prepare my heart and my spirit, to fight bravely the battles that arise in my life. And on the day of my death may your powerful presence keep me and protect me from the evil one who, in that last hour, will seek, at all costs to take my soul into the abyss where he and his legion of demons dwell. Do not leave my side! And do not allow it, O Saint Michael the Archangel, invincible warrior of God, the Most High! Amen.

46. Prayer to the Child Jesus

Holy Child Jesus, who, being true God, perfectly aware of your identity and your mission - as the best of children - submitted Yourself to the authority of the glorious Virgin Mary and Saint Joseph, her spouse, give me the gift of humility and teach me to faithfully obey those who exercise legitimate authority over me. Grant me the grace to understand that in order to enter the kingdom of heaven it is necessary to be obedient, docile and totally abandoned like a child to the will of Your heavenly Father (cf. Mt 18: 3).

To set an example, You lowered Yourself to the human condition and temporarily renounced the unlimited knowledge of all things, submitting Yourself

II Prayers to the Virgin Mary, Angels and Saints

to the historical conditions of Your existence, thus progressing in wisdom, stature and grace (cf. Lk 2: 52; CCC # 472-474). That is why I beg You to grant me the gift of being simple of heart, never proud or arrogant with the gifts and talents that I have received from You, but on the contrary, always ready to serve the less privileged (cf. Rom 12: 14).

Dispense me the grace of having a pure heart, one that is innocent and always ready to forgive. Infuse in me the same zeal and the same desire that You had in announcing the Gospel of your Father, when in the temple of Jerusalem with Your intelligence, You amazed the elders and priests who heard You speaking (cf. Lk 2: 41-52).

But above all, Blessed Child, protect all our children from all evil, from all abuse and from all kind of mistreatment. May nobody ever be allowed to steal the innocence that makes them so similar to You. Amen.

47. Prayer to our Guardian Angel

Guardian angel, friend and companion of my life, you received from God the mission of looking after me and keeping me in His grace; help me, I beg you, to persevere on the path of salvation. Forgive me for making your mission more difficult than necessary.

Prayers of the Soul

I want to thank you for your blessed assistance and I ask you to never abandon me, always protect me, and finally, when my last day in this earth comes, take my hand and guide me into the kingdom of heaven, where I will finally see face to face the One by whose command you became my custodian and my gu

III PRAYERS FOR PARTICULAR INTENTIONS

Medieval monk pensive in prayer by Thomas Mucha

III Prayers for Particular Intentions

48. Prayer for the Holy Father

Lord Jesus, supreme Shepherd of Your Church, You entrusted to Peter the mission of confirming his brothers in the true faith (cf. Lk 22: 32) and chose him from among all the Apostles to be Your Vicar on earth. We humbly ask Your help for his successor, His Holiness, Pope **N/**. Fill him with Your Holy Spirit and give him all the necessary graces to effectively fulfill the difficult mission which You have entrusted to him.

Assist him with Your Spirit so that full of knowledge and wisdom; he may be able to clearly and unambiguously teach the deposit of the true faith. Help him with Your grace so that he may ensure that Your sacraments are administered as You have established for the benefit of Your holy people. Strengthen him in Your authority so that he may govern with prudence and wisdom Your holy Church spread throughout the world and entrusted to him.

Good Shepherd, You Yourself warned Peter that the devil had asked him to shake him like wheat (cf. Lk 22: 31), protect the Holy Father so that he does not succumb to the lures of the evil one. Free him from the temptation of pride, arrogance, self-reliance, human respect, and the obsession of wanting to please the world at the expense of the Gospel. But above all, protect him against heresy and error. Help him to always keep in mind that the glory of this world passes and that the Church is not his but Yours who created her.

Lord Jesus, eternal Shepherd, we renew before You our deep love and filial obedience to Your beloved Vicar on earth and our firm confidence in Your divine words: *"… you are Peter, and on this rock I will build my Church; and the gates of Hell will not prevail against it"* (Mt 16:18) because we know that it is You Whom we listen to, when we listen to him (cf. Lk 10:16). Amen.

49. Prayer for priests

Lord Jesus, Good Shepherd, You do not abandon Your people but with love and solicitude have always provided care and nourishment. In Your wisdom You have willed to choose men from among Your people so that, clothed with Your power, they may, in Your name, make present Your holy Sacrifice through which You have saved the entire world. Listen to our prayer for our priests, especially those who work in our parish (community).

Give them a deep and unwavering love for You, so that by listening to You in their prayer You may become the center of their lives. Grant them, Lord, a profound love for Your Church in the same way a son loves his mother. May they be faithful to her holy doctrine and to the way she has always wanted to celebrate her sacraments.

Fill their hearts, Lord, with humility so that they may never preach themselves, nor their ideas, but only Your Gospel of salvation.

III Prayers for Particular Intentions

Give them, Lord, the eagerness to imitate You radically in poverty, chastity and obedience so that, by seeing them, it will be You Whom we see.

Give them too, Lord, patience so that they can lovingly accompany Your people and understand their weaknesses and their struggles.

Watch over them, Lord, so they never lack what is necessary to live a dignified life. Protect them as well from any disease, and grant them, Good Lord, the strength to resist the attacks of the evil one.

Finally, Good and Faithful Shepherd, grant them all the necessary graces to become holy priests according to Your Heart (cf. Jer 3:15) so one day, when their mission in this world ends, they may receive from You the crown of glory that does not wither (cf. 1 Cor 9: 25). We ask You this, Eternal Priest, who gloriously lives and reigns forever and ever. Amen.

50. Prayer for priests persecuted for defending the faith

Lord Jesus, eternal Priest, in order to make known Your message to us without compromises, You suffered all sort of misunderstandings and persecutions which led You to be despised, hated, tortured, and finally delivered to death on the humiliating wood of the cross.

Look with mercy on Your servants, Your priests, who, all over the world, suffer persecution and rejection in these difficult times in which Your Church finds herself. This rejection not only comes from the world, but sadly, many times also from lukewarm and confused members of Your Church, hierarchy and laity, who persecute them for their zeal and their passion to be faithful in proclaiming Your Gospel.

These beloved priests of Yours have preferred loneliness, contempt, punishment, exile, even having his sanity questioned, before trimming or diluting the Gospel that You Yourself entrusted them to preach.

Have mercy on them, Lord. Their priestly heart was modeled according to Yours, comfort them in their pains, accompany them in their loneliness, make them experience Your love in the midst of their trials, be the source of clear and pure water in the midst of their arid and inclement desert. Protect them, Lord, from their fears and their insecurities. Good Shepherd, make them know that even if everyone abandons them, You will not.

Let them experience, Lord of love and compassion, the joy of knowing that it is by Your name that they are persecuted (cf. Mt 5:11). Assure them that the world hated You before hating them (cf. Jn 15: 18). Do not let them lose sight of the unfathomable treasure that You have prepared for those who were not ashamed of proclaiming Your name before men (cf. Mk 8:38). Amen.

III Prayers for Particular Intentions

51. Prayer for priestly vocations

Lord Jesus, Good Shepherd, You have established Your Church as Your mystical body in this world and have given her the gift of the priesthood for the benefit of Your holy people. Humbly we ask You never to cease providing her with abundant priestly vocations.

We implore You to give families the necessary graces to live truly Christian lives by teaching their children to pray, to love God above all things and to obey Him always, so that these families may become fertile seedbeds of priestly vocations.

Place before young men, holy priestly witnesses, whose testimonies excite them with a life dedicated to Your service. May many young people, Lord, fall deeply in love with You and Your Gospel, give them the grace of prayer so they can hear Your voice calling them and help them to respond with generosity. Fill their hearts with the passion and the eagerness to put their lives at the service of Your people.

Give them, Lord, clear discernment in order to recognize Your voice calling them, grant them as well the gift of perfect chastity and extinguish all fear and doubt from their hearts. Infuse in their souls a sincere desire to be holy as You, Lord, are holy. We implore You to be good to Your Church, Sweet Lord, and give us holy and faithful shepherds with hearts after Yours (cf. Jer 3:15). Amen.

52. Prayer for persecuted christians

Lord Jesus, Holy Lamb who was slaughtered for our own salvation, You have asked all those who are persecuted, insulted and slandered because of Your name to rejoice because their reward will be great in heaven (cf. Mt 5: 7 -11). We ask You to have mercy on so many brothers and sisters of ours who suffer terrible and bloody persecutions in different parts of the world for the sole reason of bearing the Christian name.

Protect them, defend them, and free them from death. But if it is in Your plans that they testify to Your Gospel by shedding their blood because of their faith, give them the courage to do it with joy and resolution.

Help us to do everything possible to assist them in their needs, and to fight so that human freedom may be respected in all parts of the world and no one may be persecuted because of their religion. May the whole world come to believe in You and in Your Gospel, but never by force or violence, but by the power of the testimony and preaching of Your faithful children, and by the imperative and authoritative power of the truth. You are great Lord, and our whole life will not suffice to thank You for the gift so great that You have given us to be called Christians. Amen.

III Prayers for Particular Intentions

53. Prayer in the midst of the actual crisis in the Church

Lord Jesus, founder and faithful spouse of Your holy Church, for her You Yourself surrendered to death so that her sacraments, nourishment and support of her existence, may flow from Your open side. Look upon Your Church with mercy, now as she goes through one of the darkest chapters in her history.

In many places in the world she, called to be light, now lies in darkness; she, established as a bearer of truth, lies under the most terrible confusion; You created her to transform the world and behold, the filthy waters of this world have penetrated her sanctuary.

The situation is such that even a number of Your ministers, called to nourish and strengthen Your children, have corrupted the minds of Your faithful with ideologies and doctrines alien to Your Gospel. There have even been those who, dominated by their disordered passions and moved by the devil himself, have perpetrated against children and young people, the most defenseless of Your flock, crimes that cry out to heaven for justice.

We know that You founded the Church, that You promised to be with her always in such a way that the powers of hell would not prevail against her (cf. Mt 16:18). Intervene, Lord, with all Your power; calm the rebellious waters of this world that threaten Your Church, as You did in the boat on the stormy waters of the Sea of Galilee. Expel with Your power all the demons that have unleashed their fury on the work of Your redemption, Your holy Catholic Church.

Protect the Holy Father from the insidious attacks of the devil, free the bishops from the temptation of seeking acceptance from the world and grant Your priests the grace to live a holy life and the courage to preach the true Gospel in season and out of season (cf. 2 Tm 4: 2).

To Your laity, Lord, give the grace to recognize Your voice in the priests who speak according to Your heart, and to flee from the deceptions of the devil, who speaks through wolves dressed as shepherds. Give every faithful catholic hunger to know the true faith, the one faith that does not change and for which thousands of men and women gave their lives in order to defend.

Do not allow, Lord, any of Your children to succumb to the temptation to leave the true and only Church because of the scandal of Your ministers. One day, not too far away, Lord, may clergy and laity together contemplate again fully and diaphanous the beautiful face of Your Church in all her splendor and glory as You thought of her and loved her even before the foundation of the world. Amen.

III Prayers for Particular Intentions

54. Prayer for the evangelization of the peoples

Lord Jesus, unfailing light of all that exists, we adore You, praise You and thank You for calling us out of the darkness of ignorance and sin to Your admirable and ineffable light (cf. Col 1:13). You, on the day of Your ascension to heaven, commanded Your Apostles: *"Go, and make disciples of all nations, baptizing them in the name of the Father, and of the Son, and of the Holy Spirit; teaching them to keep all that I have commanded you"* (Mt 28: 19-20). From that moment and through the centuries Your holy Church - created to evangelize - has unceasingly labored so that the good news of Your Word can reach all the ends of the earth. Help us, we ask You, to redouble our efforts so that no man or woman on the face of the earth leaves this world without hearing the announcement of Your Gospel.

We recognize that those who do not know You are indeed capable of knowing You to the degree You have revealed Yourself through Your creation (cf. CCC # 36). Neither do we ignore that among them there are good people who carry Your law in their hearts and who seek You with a sincere heart. We also know that in their cultures exist positive elements; "seeds" placed there by Your hands (cf. St. Justin) to better dispose them to the reception of Your Gospel. For all this, Lord, we give You thanks.

However, we do not ignore -because You have taught us so- that due to sin present in all human beings, without the knowledge of Your revelation, humanity throughout history as a whole, has lost its way replacing Your ineffable glory with images of the creatures found in the very nature that surrounds them. Satan, the enemy of the human race, very often, taking advantage of their ignorance, enslaves them through lies, pushing them, even now, to commit atrocities against each other, bringing death and destruction upon themselves and their children (cf. Rom 1: 19-32).

Help us to carry Your good news to all the peoples of the earth. May everyone know You, accept You and be reborn in the waters of baptism so that, transformed into Your disciples, they may enjoy the freedom that comes from being God's children through You (cf. Rom 8:21) in the bosom of Your holy Church outside of which there is no salvation (cf. CCC # 846). We confess this with deep joy because we know that only in Your name there is redemption and that *"... there is no other name under heaven, given to men, in which we can be saved"* (Acts 4:12).

We thank You for so many men and women who, leaving everything behind, embarked into unknown worlds and cultures with the sole purpose of making Your name known to all. These great evangelists knew how to take Your Word to these nations with respect, kindness and generosity, enriching these cultures not only with the Gospel, but also with prosperity and development. Some of them even shed

III Prayers for Particular Intentions

their own blood, becoming in this way seeds of new Christians.

On the other hand, we do not ignore that in the past some children of Your Church, driven not by Gospel values, but by power, money and desire for domination, failed to bear witness to Your love, committing crimes that have left shadows and wounds in the evangelization of many peoples. Forgive us, Lord, never let the proclamation of Your Gospel ever be mixed with injustices, slavery and death. May all who believe in You do so in freedom without which there can be no faith.

Give us, then, evangelizers with burning hearts for Your love, capable of leaving everything behind and entering into the most remote places and assist them in the mission You gave them of saving souls. Give them wisdom to present Your message in the best possible way, so that those who hear it can understand and accept it. Give them courage not to fear the dangers and threats of those who do not want to let the Gospel resonate in every corner of the earth. Protect them from every evil, and free them from discouragement and fatigue. O Lord do not let them ever be ashamed of Your Gospel (cf. Rom 1:16) by following wrong ideologies and theologies that do not recognize You as the beginning and the end of all evangelization. Hence, with humility and passion for the salvation of souls, we beseech You, O Lord, to help Your Church to proclaim Your redemption to every corner of the world so that *"... all men may be saved and come to the knowledge of the truth"* (1 Tim 2: 4). Amen.

55. Prayer for christian unity

Lord God, Father, Son and Holy Spirit, perfect and unbreakable unity in a diversity of persons, when the fullness of time came, the Second Person of Your Trinity, the Eternal Logos, became man so that in Your name He would unify the human race in a single people born of Your love, partaking of a single baptism, believing one faith, under the staff of one shepherd and gathered in one Spirit (cf. Eph 4: 5-7).

You, Eternal Father, teach us that this perfect unity remains to this day in the holy Catholic Church. We know, however, that this unity is always threatened not only by our fragile human condition, but above all by the insidious attacks of the Devil, the enemy of our race. Indeed, already on the very night of Your Son's Passion, it was by the inspirations of the devil that Your disciples were frightened and dispersed (cf. Mt 26:31), it was also him who seduced Judas into betraying Your Son (cf. Lk 22: 3) and it was him as well who pushed Peter to deny Him three times (cf. Mt 26: 69-75). Full of anger, however, for his failure, at that time, to ruin Your work of salvation, he continued to tempt Your Son's disciples throughout history in order to divide Your Church.

Before entering into His passion, Your Son raised His prayer to You, Eternal Father, for all of us,

III Prayers for Particular Intentions

who by the word of His apostles would believe one day in His message, so that we may be one, just like You with Him and the Holy Spirit are One (cf. Jn 17: 21-23). You heard, O Lord, this prayer from Your beloved Son and kept intact the unity of Your Church throughout the centuries. However, some of Your children, pushed, not only by the enemy, but many times, also by our bad example, decided to break away from the perfect communion established by You in Your Church. Thus, throughout history and moving further and further away from Your flock, these men founded other communities that, even though, still bear the name Christian, no longer enjoy the fullness of faith and the unity that You wished for Your holy Church since her foundation.

Have mercy on all of us and to us who still profess the fullness of faith within Your one Church, grant true love for those who have left, so we can always see them, despise this situation, as true brothers and sisters. Help us to rejoice in those elements of salvation which we still share with them. Teach us to be humble to recognize the mistakes and sins that have been committed and that we continue to commit against the unity of the Church of Your Son which prevent unity from being achieved.

Lord, bring back home those who are separated from perfect communion, and help them to understand that it was always Your will to have only one Church, gathered around a single Shepherd. May they realize that the Church is not our property, to create or transform it at our whim, but the property of Your Son who wanted a Church in all its glory, without spot, or wrinkle, or anything like that (cf. Eph 5:27). That one day, in not too great a distance, respecting the historical traditions that You, in Your wisdom, allowed to arise outside the physical borders of Your family, may we, Christians, all meet again in the profession of a single faith in the bosom of Your holy Catholic and Apostolic Church. That in this Church may we all praise You under a single staff, that of Your Son present in the person of His Vicar on earth, the Holy Father, and of all the pastors of the entire world in communion with him. We ask all this through Your Son Jesus Christ Our Lord in Whom we all are one. Amen.

56. Prayer for peace

Lord Jesus, Prince of peace, You came to this world to bring harmony among all men who love God (Lk 2:14), today we ask You to pour out abundantly this same peace throughout the whole world.

In today's world men have moved away from You searching for a prosperity that is purely human. They have forgotten that only in the fulfillment of Your mandates, can we all achieve a true development, one that can help us to find real happiness.

III Prayers for Particular Intentions

Have mercy on this world, Lord, in which too often man raises his hand against his own brother, exactly as at the beginning of history (cf. Gen 4: 8). Many innocent people suffer because of these confrontations as a result of ambition, selfishness and corruption.

Hatred between races, social classes, ideologies and even religions destroys lives and leads entire nations into desolation and annihilation. Very often the world ignores that all men, created in Your image and likeness, have the same dignity before You, and that it is Your will that we all love and respect one another in this world in an environment of harmony and cooperation.

Send to all men's hearts, especially those in government and to political and religious leaders, the necessary graces to promote peace. May the innocent no longer die, may there be enough bread for all and may every useless confrontation cease. May dialogue, concord and reason find their way through the forces of division, hatred and revenge.

But above all we humbly ask You to make every man and every woman understand that only in You, absolute Truth, can there be true peace, not as the world gives it (Jn 14:27), but a lasting one, the only kind capable of being the foundation of a prosperous and fair human society. Amen.

57. Prayer for immigrants

Lord, God of our fathers, You called Abraham and asked him -in his old age- to leave the security of his paternal house to travel to a distant land, a land promised by You to him and to his offspring (cf. Gn 12: 1). Later, You Yourself, rescued Moses from the waters of the Nile (cf. Ex 2: 5-7) so that freeing Your people from the yoke of Pharaoh, he could lead them into the Promised Land, a land from which milk and honey flowed (cf. 3: 8). To fulfill Your promise, You instructed him to take Your people into the desert where You purified them and worked on their behalf great portents against his enemies (cf. 17).

In the fullness of time, when Your beloved Son dwelt among us, You ordered Joseph, Your servant, to take the child and His mother and flee from the murderous wrath of Herod into Egypt, where Your Son was an immigrant and knew what it was like to live in a culture different from His (cf. Mt 14:19).

Look kindly to all those who, due to different circumstances, leave their homes, their loved ones, their countries and their cultures to undertake a journey, often dangerous, in search of a better future for themselves and their families.

We humbly ask You to bless them, Lord, You who know the difficulties of their lives, bless their journey and protect them, free them from all kinds of slavery, trafficking and violence and make them reach their destination safely and with health. Provide them with decent work, make them feel welcome and accepted and give them the wisdom to adapt and assimilate to their new circumstances.

III Prayers for Particular Intentions

Do not let believers lose their faith in their path. And to those who do not believe, help them, Lord, to realize Your loving presence in their journey. That none of them be content to seek only goods that perish, but those that come from above (cf. Jn 6:27). Provide their families left behind what is necessary for their sustenance and procure that in the near future they may be reunited. Your Son was a stranger in a foreign land, have mercy on those who are now traveling in search of a better future. Amen.

58. Prayer for the sick

Lord Jesus, You are the fullness of the human race, You have not wanted death or disease to exist, but instead, You have destined us to live forever and have endowed our body with health and well-being. But it was because of sin that death and disease were introduced into the world (cf. Rom 5:12). In Your mercy, though, You have willed to come to our aid, becoming a man so through Your flesh and Your wounds You may heal us (cf. Is 53: 5). Look, hence, with compassion to all who suffer under the yoke of disease. I especially ask You for ... *(mention the name of the sick people to whom you want to pray)*.

Give them patience so that they do not despair, give them courage to accept their pains, give them strength to endure their sufferings, and give them a supernatural sight in order to know that their sufferings have a profound meaning and a reason in Your plan of salvation.

Give them last, Lord, if it is for Your greatest glory and for the salvation of their souls, the ultimate cure of all their diseases so that with their brothers and sisters they may continue to praise You in health, spiritually and physically, during the remaining time of their mortal lives. Amen.

59. Prayer of a mother for the conversion of her children

My Lord and my God, loving and merciful Father, have pity and compassion on my children who have turned away from You and today are walking on the wide path that leads to perdition (cf. Mt 7: 3).

It was You who gave them to me and in Your name, I tried to provide them, in the midst of my limitations, not only the material good they needed, but also and above all, a spiritual life and a deep love for You.

But You created us free and when they grew up, like the prodigal son, they left Your house and Your gifts, choosing to stray from Your commandments.

III Prayers for Particular Intentions

Although they are my children and the fruits of my womb, I know very well that my love for them is a drop in the ocean compared to the love that You, Good Lord, have for them since You created them for love and redeemed them by the shedding of Your precious Blood. Have compassion on them, I beseech You!

Give them the necessary graces to find the truth, save them from sudden death, change their unrepentant hearts, make them find You again and straighten their paths so they may love You with all their being and may follow You faithfully again.

Keep them from bad company, from vices and from their disorderly passions. Infuse in their hearts a deep love for Your mysteries so that they may return to Your Church, the paternal house. In this way, once they have come back to You, their minds and their wills may focus on working day by day with fear and trembling in the salvation of their souls and for the establishment of Your kingdom in this world (cf. Phil 2:12).

I humbly ask You to accept my sufferings, my prayers, my sacrifices and everything I can do so that the children of my many tears may not be lost. Good and patient God hear my prayer for these children of mine who in Your mercy You entrusted to my care and whom I place now under Your kind protection with the certain hope that one day with them I will be found worthy of gazing at the beauty of Your countenance for all eternity. Amen.

60. Prayer for children suffering under extreme poverty

Lord, friend and companion of our lives, You instructed Your disciples not to prevent children from approaching You, teaching them that of those who are like them belong the kingdom of heaven (cf. Lk 9:48).

I ask You for those children, so many of them, who today suffer worldwide poverty, misery, hunger, lack of education, abuse and exploitation. Have mercy on all of them, they are Your children, so close to Your Heart.

You Yourself wanted to become a child, be born in poverty and, although innocent, You were hated and persecuted, to the point that You had to flee Your homeland and live part of Your childhood in a foreign country (cf. Mt 2: 14).

Look at all these children with compassion, protect them, defend them, and deliver them from all evil. That food, education, in short, all the tools they need to grow healthy and strong, may always be available to them.

But above all, Lord, make them know You and love You, and may their souls be saved. Help all of us to fight for a more just world where no child shall suffer the horrors of misery and hunger. We ask all this of You

III Prayers for Particular Intentions

Whom as a child wanted to enter into this world bringing with You true peace and countless blessings. Amen.

61. Prayer for an extremely ill child

Lord, God of life, You are the source of compassion and kindness. You have said: *'Let the children come to me"* (Mt 9:14). And You were filled with tenderness to see them and play with them. You felt so happy with them, no doubt, because of their innocence and simplicity which sadly many of us lose as we grow up. That is why You have also said that of those who are like them is the kingdom of heaven (cf. Mt 18, 3).

You Yourself, Lord, took pity on Jairus who begged You to come to his house to cure his little girl who lay in bed seriously ill (cf. Mc 5: 21-42). At another time, also, encouraging us to pray without ceasing, You said to us: *"If you, being bad, know how to give good gifts to your children, how much more will your Father in heaven give good things to those who ask Him?"* (Mt 7: 11).

With deep confidence in these words, we humbly come to ask You for **N/**. Who suffers under the burden of this terrible illness. Lord, if we who are evil feel so moved by this little one, we are sure that You, infinite Goodness, feel for him (her), for whom You shed Your Blood and whose innocence pleases You so much, deepest compassion.

Have mercy on him (her), Lord, relieve his (her) pains, mitigate his (her) sufferings, grant him (her) health, heal him (her), we beg You with profound humility.

We have offended You and carry the burden of our faults, but this little one, although our son (daughter) and member of our human race, has no fault of his (her) own. Have mercy on him (her), Lord, for the sake of Your Passion, for the sake of Your cross, for the sake of Your most holy Mother, for the sake of Your love of Your Father in heaven, do not ignore our pleas for **N/.** who suffers under the cruel yoke of disease. Amen.

62. Prayer for the death of a baptized child

Lord Jesus, God of love and consolation, before You we come with deep pain for the death of **N/.** In Your unyielding wisdom, You have allowed this child, whose birth filled us with joy, to leave now our side plunging us into deep sadness and desolation. Why does an innocent have to suffer and die? Why does a little creature's life have to be extinguished so soon by the cold breath of death? So many questions, Lord, come to our minds and to our hearts because of the death of this innocent little one. The answers are mysteriously hidden in the cross of Your Beloved Son who, being innocent suffered and die for our salvation. From the darkness of our humanity and filled with pain and grief, we want to confess that *"... we have believed that You are the Christ, the Son of God, even He who comes into the world." (Jn 11: 27)*.

That is why today we come before You, so that by faith in You our tears may be wiped away and through hope in You, our hearts may be comforted. We thank You, however, because **N/.** could be reborn in the waters of baptism and that comforts us greatly. Indeed, Lord, our

III Prayers for Particular Intentions

faith consoles us with the certainty that this little one, redeemed with Your grace, is already enjoying Your eternal glory. It comforts us to know that he (she) no longer suffers, but on the contrary, he (she) now enjoys a happiness that cannot be expressed in words. Indeed, now he (she) is witnessing what *"eye has not seen, nor ear heard, nor have entered into the heart of man about the things which God has prepared for those who love Him"* (cf. 1 Cor 2:9). How much peace this certainty brings to our hearts!

His (her) departure, however, leaves us also with deep sadness, especially to his parents. Therefore, Lord, You who took pity on the sadness of the widow from Nain who was about to bury her son (cf. Lk 7: 11-17), and on Jairus' tears, when he found his little girl dead (cf. 8: 49-50), we ask You, with humility and confidence, to have mercy on the parents and the family of this little one. Comfort them and console them in the hope that they will see their son (daughter) again in Your kingdom of glory. And to those of us who remain in this world, help us not to lose the purity and holiness that You have given us back with Your grace through our baptism and strengthen our hope that one day we will meet in heaven with **N/.** under whose intercession we now entrust ourselves. Amen.

63. Prayer for the death of an unbaptized child

Lord Jesus, God of love and consolation, before You we come with deep pain for the death of **N/.** In Your unyielding wisdom You have allowed this child, whose birth filled us with joy, to leave now our side plunging us into deep sadness and desolation. Why does an innocent have to suffer and die? Why does a little creature's life have to be extinguished so soon by the cold breath of death? So many questions, Lord, come to our minds and to our hearts because of the death of this innocent little one. The answers are mysteriously hidden in the cross of Your Beloved Son who, being innocent suffered and died for our salvation. From the darkness of our humanity and filled with pain and grief, we want to confess that *"... we have believed that You are the Christ, the Son of God, even He who comes into the world." (Jn 11: 27)*.

The circumstances did not allow us to take him (her) to the baptismal font for which he (she) left this world as one of Your most beautiful creatures, but not as Your son (daughter), partaker of Your divine life and hence, heir of Your heavenly kingdom. But we believe in Your infinite mercy and Your predilection for children, and since he (she) could not become You child to no fault of his (her) own, we trust that by means known only by You, You will send him (her) the necessary graces to be saved and fully enjoy Your glorious kingdom.

His (her) departure also leaves us, especially his (her) parents, with deep sadness. Therefore, Lord, You who took pity on the widow of Nain, who was about to bury his son (cf. Lk 7: 11-17) and on Jairus, who weep disheartening when he learned that his little girl had already died (cf. Lk 8: 49-50), we ask You to take pity on the parents and the family of this little one. Comfort them and console them in the hope of seeing their son (daughter) again in Your kingdom of glory. And to those of us who remain in this world, help us not to lose the innocence that You have given us back with Your grace through our baptism. Accept, therefore, Lord, our prayers

III Prayers for Particular Intentions

and our supplications for the soul of little **N/.** to whom we entrust to Your infinite mercy. Amen.

64. Prayer for the end of abortion

Lord Jesus, God of life and innocence, have mercy and compassion on us. We come to You with a heavy heart to beg You to change the hearts of this perverse generation which destroys the lives of their unborn children, the most innocent and the most defenseless. This generation, in defiance of Your authority, has transformed the mother's womb from a sacrosanct source of life, into a chamber of death and destruction.

Heed our pleas and take pity on these innocent souls who return to You rejected by this world. We ask You to touch the hearts of every politician and those who can change this horrendous situation so that they see the atrocity, the monstrosity and the abomination of what has become the worst crime of our time.

Fill with Your Spirit the minds of those mothers who are contemplating the possibility of abortion, heal with Your loving and forgiving hand the hearts of those who have already done so. Convert and forgive those who promote it endlessly. Remind the doctors of the oath they made of never ending, nor harming a human life.

You, Lord, are the Supreme Shepherd of the Church; unfortunately, inside Your Church there have also emerged shepherds who have betrayed the Gospel and seek to silence the defense of life. Do not let the Church be silent before this injustice. Send us true shepherds after Your own heart and grant comfort and strengthen those priests who suffer persecution for preaching against the horrendous crime of abortion.

That soon, Lord, this unjust law, wherever it has been past, which allows mothers to kill their babies, may be a bitter chapter in the memory of history. Grant all of us to always welcome all unborn babies either wanted or not wanted, healthy or sick, loved or not, with open arms, and help us to always remember that by welcoming a child in Your name, it is You Whom we welcome (cf. Lk 9: 48), O God of life and innocence. Amen.

65. Prayer to be said outside the abortion chambers

Lord Jesus, almighty and eternal God, to You the heavens, the earth and the abyss sing Your praises. Before Your power and wisdom there is no human or spiritual entity that can resist You (cf. Phil 2: 10). Today we ask You to assist us in our difficult mission. It was You, in Your goodness, who called us to save the lives of these babies. They are beautiful creatures of Yours, innocent little ones whom in these times have especially become prey to the ferocity of the enemy of the human race that reigns and operates in this factory of death. We are aware of the words of the Apostle: *"For our struggle is not against flesh and blood, but against the rulers, against the authorities, against the powers of this dark world and against the spiritual forces of evil in the heavenly realms"* (Eph. 6: 12).

III Prayers for Particular Intentions

That is why we ask You, Lord, to put on us the full armor of God, so that when the day of evil comes, we may be able to stand our ground. Help us to stand firm with the belt of truth buckled around our waist, with the breastplate of righteousness in place, and with our feet fitted with the readiness that comes from the Gospel of peace (cf. Eph 6: 13-15).

Behold in this building, Lord, the prince of this world reigns, he, like in times of Herod (cf. Mt 2:16), not only claims the lives of these innocent little ones in sacrifice, but has enslaved men and women who blinded by his lies, serve him with great promptness and efficiency. Here today many confused women, enslaved by the darkness of sin will come pursuing to end the life they carry in their wombs. Do not allow it, Lord!

Give us, Good Father, the words and the appropriate gesture so that those women with whom we will speak may see in us love and not condemnation. Touch their hearts, open their eyes, and make the children in their wombs, growing so close to their hearts cling to hers so that they feel from within, especially today, the voice of supplication of the innocent life which You are forming inside of them. To us, Your servants give us the courage not to be afraid or to be intimidated by insults and threats. Protect us, Lord, from all physical and spiritual evil.

To the doctors, nurses and staff who work in this center, flood them with Your grace, show them the darkness in which they live, make them realize their errors and stop them from continuing to cooperate with the holocaust of these babies. May today, Lord, no child may be executed within these walls. With Your power, make the devil and his angels flee from this place and be thrown into hell from where they should never have escaped. May these little creatures of Yours grow with normality and health, be born to this life and to Your grace, so that after praising You in their earthly existence, they may deserve to eternally enjoy Your glory in heaven.

And to those children who will die today, despite our efforts and prayers, we ask You to reach them with the grace of Your salvation. We trust that You will take care of them and that You will receive them back in an infinite and merciful embrace filled with tenderness and love. Once in Your bosom, after welcoming them into heaven, make them hear from Your mouth, as a lullaby of infinite love, those beautiful words of Yours spoken of by the prophet Isaiah *"Can a mother forget the baby at her breast and have no compassion on the child she has borne? Though she may forget, I will not forget you!"* (Is 49: 15). Amen.

66. Prayer for the soul of someone who committed suicide

Lord of justice and God of mercy. *"My heart is full of misfortune and my life is on the edge of the abyss"* (Ps 88: 4). It is in this way that I humbly approach You today in order to implore You for the soul of **N/.**

In Your holy presence, I want to confess my faith that You and only You are the Lord of life and that our poverty is so great that we do not even own our lives (cf. CCC # 2280). For that reason, putting an end to our existence by our own hand in all circumstances,

III Prayers for Particular Intentions

objectively speaking, is a very great offense against Your divine majesty.

But You are Good and Merciful, Lord, and nothing that is in the heart of man is hidden from You (cf. Prv 15:11; Jer 20:11; Mt 12: 25; Lk 6:8). You, better than anyone, understand the difficult circumstances to which human beings are often exposed, and do not ignore that many times there are psychological conditions that can limit and even nullify our freedom and our ability to decide (cf. CCC # 2282). Because of all this, we know that only You and no one but You can judge someone who decides to take his (her) own life. For this reason, I ask You to have mercy on Your son (daughter) **N/.** And forgive all his (her) sins.

Comfort those who mourn his (her) tragic death today, inspire us to always pray for him (her), so that, without relativizing the seriousness of this decision, we never lose hope in Your mercy and in his (her) salvation (cf. CCC # 2283).

And to all of us, we humbly ask You to help us to be more attentive to the problems and pains of those who suffer in silence and loneliness their tragedies and misfortunes. Help us bring hope and faith where there is despair and darkness. Let all know, Good and Gracious God, that for You there is nothing impossible and that even death has been defeated by the resurrection of Your beloved Son. In Him, You have shown us Your infinite love and Your will that all men be saved (cf. 1 Tim 2: 4) and that none of those whom You gave to Your Son be lost (cf. Jn 18: 9). Amen.

67. Prayer for our enemies

Lord Jesus, God of love and reconciliation, You have taught us that there is nothing extraordinary in loving those who love us and doing good to our benefactors. On the contrary, You have told us that the greatness of being Your disciples consists in loving our enemies and praying for those who seek our destruction (cf. Mt 5: 43-48). You have taught us this, not only with Your words, but with Your own actions when from the cross You Yourself asked forgiveness for those who crucified You (cf. Lk 23: 34).

That is why I beg You to grant me the grace to follow Your example, make my heart capable of such a great gesture of love and generosity. Listen to my prayer for my enemies and for those who had and even now do wish me evil. Help me to feel compassion for them, to always be willing to shake their hand, to love them and to wish them good. Change their hearts so that they may be pleasing to You, by the power of Your Divine Grace, save their souls, bless their families, protect them and grant that one day they and I can praise You forever in the kingdom of peace and of Your eternal glory. Amen.

68. Prayer for our friends

Lord Jesus, You have willed to call us no longer servants, but Your friends, since You have revealed to us everything that Your Father has entrusted to You (cf.

III Prayers for Particular Intentions

Jn 15:15). Today I humbly ask You to watch over all my friends, those who accompanied me in the past and that even now continue to accompany me in my life. You have told us: *"Behold, how good and how pleasant it is for brethren to dwell together in unity!"* (Ps 133: 1) and also that *"whoever finds a friend finds a treasure"* (Sir 6: 14).

Strengthen, therefore, I ask You, the bonds of closeness, loyalty and charity that I have with all my friends, that through our friendship, we may always search for You. Inspire us to know the best way to exercise fraternal correction among us and never allow any of us to depart from You. Make us true friends, not only rejoicing during times of fortune, but above all, helping each other during moments of darkness and suffering. Shed Your grace abundantly, Lord, upon all my friends, always graciously hear their prayers, and protect their families from the evil one and from every evil. Make us one in Your love so that one day - they and I - may enjoy Your friendship in Your kingdom of love and brotherhood. Amen.

69. Prayer for intercession for those who ask to pray for them

Almighty and merciful God, I am not a just man (woman) therefore my prayer is not that powerful and pleasing before You (cf. Ja 5:16), nor am I always faithful to Your commands so I can deserve to be heard by You. I have confidence, however, in what

Your beloved Son taught us: *"So far you have asked for nothing in my name; ask, and you will receive, that your joy may be complete"* (Jn 16:24). Encouraged by these divine words, today I come before You, in the name of Jesus, to intercede for those who entrust themselves to my humble prayers, bless them, Lord, and assist them in their needs.

I ask You for my family, grant them the grace to know You and love You. Look at my friends with kindness, so that their friendship with You may become even stronger. For the sick, I ask, so that You, Lord, may heal them, comfort them and give them patience. For those who feel lonely, help them experience Your company. For all those marriages that experience problems and difficulties I beg You that they may discover Your love and the power through Your grace dwelling in them. For my benefactors, reward them for their generosity. For priests, make them holy and brave in their mission. For the dying, assist them so that they may be prepared to meet You with all the means of salvation that You have placed in Your Church to their disposal.

Receive, Lord, my poor, but no less fervent prayer, and make me holy and perfect as You are holy and perfect (cf. Mt 5:48), so that my life may be pleasing to You, Good God, and may You be pleased in listening to my prayers, especially on behalf of those who ask for my humble intercession. Amen.

III Prayers for Particular Intentions

70. Prayer for creation

God and Creator of the universe, only in You there is absolute perfection and only in You the source of all beauty can be found. I thank You for all that You have created, for the heavens, the earth, the sea, the lakes, the rivers, the mountains, the valleys, as well as for all the animals and beasts in the oceans and on the face of the earth. Everything You have created bears witness to Your majesty, Your strength, Your greatness and Your beauty.

You gave us the mandate to fill and subdue the earth (cf. Gn 1:28), but You never gave us a license to abuse it, mistreat it, much less to prey on it in order to satisfy our greed and our excessive ambition. For not having taken care of nature we humbly ask for Your forgiveness.

We thank You also because in us, human beings, You have manifested the highest perfection of all Your creation. In Your wisdom You willed to give us an intelligence superior to that of animals in order to dominate creation and subdue it. Moreover, in our own nature, in a mysterious way, You also gave us an immortal soul, called to share Your own divine nature in such a way that in us all creation is elevated to a higher destiny.

Because of our disobedience, however, we subjected all of creation to a state of death, which is why she groans until today with labor pains awaiting her release (cf. Rom 8: 22). But if our sins reduced her to such a dramatic state, our reconciliation with You, God of majesty and goodness, has launched her rescue. With this You teach us that no one can value and care for creation as much as those who have been reconciled to You through Your beloved Son, *"the first born of all creation"* (Col 1: 5).

Inspire, then, each man and each woman to value nature in its depth, and to be aware that by destroying it we not only destroy Your work, but also, we destroy ourselves. We need creation for our subsistence in this world and creation depends on us for its deliverance from sin and death. In this way all creation sings joyfully Your glory and Your praise (cf. Ps 148). Help us, then, to join her in that song of joy so that one day we all may contemplate the new heavens and the new earth that You have prepared for those who have been rescued in Christ Jesus (cf. Rev 21: 1). Amen.

71. Prayer for our Nation

Heavenly Father, God of love and consolation, by commanding us to honor our parents, You want us also to love and honor the land in which You willed to give us life. That is why we ask You today

III Prayers for Particular Intentions

to bless our country. Free our nation from natural disasters, epidemics, invasions and wars. Never abandon us to secularism, atheism, communism, racism, civil wars and dictatorships. In a word, protect us against everything that prevents us from being a nation worthy of praising Your name and living according to Your mandates.

Respecting the freedom of each of our citizens, may our country always be willing to recognize Your dominion and Your power. Deliver us from the tragedy of putting our laws against Yours. May we never call good what You have taught us to call evil and evil what You have shown us is good. Bless our land with justice for all, rich and poor alike, as well as for all minorities. Especially may the poorest of the poor find in our homeland food and shelter. Bless our children, take care of our youth and guard our elders. Free our authorities from corruption and provide decent jobs to every person living within our borders.

Finally, always help us to welcome the foreigner and also share our wealth with those people less fortunate than us, or those who go through rough times. Protect those who have dedicated their lives to the defense of our country and have mercy on those who already shed their blood so that we can live in freedom. May we one day, together, enjoy perfect happiness in the eternal homeland of Your glory. All this, Good Lord, we ask in the name of Jesus, our Lord and our King. Amen.

72. Prayer for the end of a pandemia

Lord Jesus, Doctor and Healer of our souls and our bodies, we ask You today with deep faith to have mercy on us all and on the whole world, especially during this time of pandemia

You did not create disease, suffering, or death, but these came as a consequence of humanity's sin. In Your wisdom, however, You wanted to endow all human suffering with a supernatural meaning and turn it into a vehicle of salvation, so that pain, illness and even death can serve as a way of return when, forgetting about You, we give ourselves to the pleasures of this world.

We know, Lord, that despite our miseries and sins You do not abandon us to our fate, but constantly and in many ways, You call us to conversion. Your love for the whole world compelled You to send down Your own Son (cf. Jn 3:16), clothed with our own flesh thus, becoming like us in all things but sin. In this way Your Son, sharing Your divinity, was able to experience pain, illness, suffering and even death in order to save us from evil.

Turn, therefore, O God of love and salvation, Your compassionate and kind countenance on the face of the earth and gaze upon the entire world that today groans under the yoke of this terrible and mortal pandemia. By Your power and by Your mercy, deliver us from this evil plague that spreads at a speed never seen before. You who have power over the forces of nature, raise Your mighty

III Prayers for Particular Intentions

arm and make this virus flee and thus, stop extinguishing the lives of so many innocent people.

God of mercy and goodness, we ask You with deep humility to heal the sick, watch especially over the elderly and children, send Your angels to protect the doctors and nurses who risk their lives seeking to alleviate the pain of their brothers and sisters. O Lord, by Your precious Blood shed on the cross, make this pandemia stop now.

But, above all, Lord of Justice, make all men and women, all nations, peoples and cultures, even Your own Church, open their eyes to see that by seeking first Your Kingdom and its justice, everything else, including physical health, will be granted to them (cf. Mt 6.33). Therefore, do not allow us, like Pharaoh, to continue hardening our hearts, but help us to believe in You and follow You faithfully (cf. Ex 9, 7). Mary, help of Christians, Angels and saints of God pray for us during these difficult and dangerous times. Amen.

IV PRAYERS IN PARTICULAR CIRCUMSTANCES

Zaragoza, Spain. The painting of Michael Archangel in the Church of the Exaltación de la Santa Cruz by Manuel Eraso. March 2, 2018:

IV Prayers in Particular Circumstances

73. Prayer for employment

Lord Jesus, God with us, from the beginning of Your human life, Your Father entrusted You to the care of Saint Joseph, and under his tutelage You learned the importance of human work, as well as the dignity that gives man the power to earn his bread by the sweat of his brow (cf. Gen 3:19). You, who grew up in a foreign country a firsthand witness to Joseph's many efforts to find employment as an immigrant in order to provide sustenance for You and Your holy Mother.

Look with compassion on my family and on me, Your most humble servant. I am in great need of finding a good job, one that is dignifying, well-paid and stable, so that I can feed my children, and provide for them as Your Father, God provident, provide for all creation (cf. Ps 65: 9-13).

Finding a job can be a very long, frustrating and time-consuming process, give me thus, Lord, patience and humility to persevere and not give up. Grant me wisdom and help me to be well prepared for the job interviews that I have ahead of me. I trust, Lord, that You, just and generous as You always are with me, will listen to my confident plea which I present to You with deep faith. I know that, by Your kindness, You will attend soon to my request.

But above all, Lord, I ask You with deep fervor - whether in need or in abundance – never allow me or anyone in my family to be separated from You, since away from You, there is neither prosperity nor happiness. I present this petition trusting in the powerful intercession of Saint Joseph, Patron saint of workers. Amen.

74. Prayer at the beginning of work

Lord God and Creator of all that exists, Your creation is full of greatness and wonders. My heart gives You thanks, especially because in this creation, You have wanted to make all men participants and co-creators of the work of Your hands.

When the fullness of time arrived, You sent Your beloved Son to announce to us the good news of salvation and to sacrifice his life to redeem us. But before doing all of these, He wanted to learn how to work as a man under the guidance of Your servant Saint Joseph thus, earning his livelihood with the sweat of his brow (cf. Gen 3:19).

Before I begin my work, I implore You with deep humility for the grace of not working only for the things that perish, but for those that last forever (cf. Jn 6:27). Even though I am a useless servant (cf. Lk 17:10), assist me with Your help so my work may cooperate in my own salvation, while glorifying You before all men.

Give me the strength that I need, as well as the power and energy to mitigate and relieve my tiredness. Do not let me hurt myself or others in the execution of my work. Give my hands and my intelligence the perfection that comes from You, so that the fruit of my effort bears witness to Your greatness and cooperates in the construction of a better and more just world. Amen.

IV Prayers in Particular Circumstances

75. Prayer at the end of work

Lord Jesus, friend and companion on my journey, You said *"Come to me, all you who are weary and burdened, and I will give you rest"* (Mt 11:28), at the end of this workday, I beg You to relieve my tiredness while I thank You for my job, through which I am able to support my family.

I also want to thank You for keeping me healthy which allows me to work. By Your grace do not let me lack health and work. I thank You too because being united with You by Your grace, everything that I did today, has not only served the well-being and material development of human beings, but also has contribute it to my own salvation. Forgive me, Lord, if I did not work with the perfection and dedication I should have. Tomorrow I will try to do better. Thank You for the successes and achievements I accomplished today, Good God, they are Your gift.

Now that I return home, help me to appreciate and enjoy my wife (husband) and my children. Do not let my tiredness and my worries make me indifferent, cold, and, much less, rude to them. You worked hard in Your mortal life and that is why I know You understand my tiredness very well. Have mercy on me and never let me depart from You. Lord Jesus may Your name be blessed and praised in each one of my actions and throughout my whole life. Amen.

76. Prayer of a student

Lord Jesus, infinite wisdom, before You I come with deep humility to ask You to shed light on my mind and on my intelligence.

Lord, You have willed to endow us with intelligence in order to scrutinize the mysteries of nature that surrounds us - and of which we are part - so that by dominating it, always with respect and care, we can use it for our own benefit and for the benefit of the entire world.

You have also given our intelligence the capacity to know that You exist, that You are One and are interested in us (cf. CCC # 35-36). You have also wanted to make us capable of faith, as a form of knowledge that does not contradict our reason but rather, helps and perfects it to know those truths that we could not access by our sole intelligence.

Send, then, upon me, Your Spirit of wisdom and knowledge, that through his power, my intelligence might overcome the effects of sin and those of my own ignorance. Let it illuminate my memory, my capacity of reflection, abstraction, logic and my practical ability to focus, learn and retain what I am about to study. With Your help and assistance, I know that I will be able to improve myself in this specific field of science (technology, discipline) to which I have dedicated myself.

Moreover, Lord, grant that I not only understand what I need to learn at the human level, but that this

IV Prayers in Particular Circumstances

knowledge may always lead me to want to know You more so I can love You, serve You and live according to Your mandates. The end of the human mind is the Truth and the only absolute Truth is You, eternal Word, by Whom the whole universe was made and in whose light everything that exists finds its explanation (cf. Jn 1:1). Amen.

77. Prayer of blessing of a mother to her child
(Cf. 2 Mc 7: 22-23)

My child, I do not know how you appeared in my womb; it was not me who gave you life and breath, nor was it I who organized your body. It was the Creator of the world, who did all things, Who formed you in my bosom from the first moment. May this same God in His infinite mercy protect you, make the light of His face shine upon you, may He never let you depart from His commandments and grant you someday the grace to enjoy the glory of His kingdom. *(Making the sign of the cross on her son or daughter the mother process to bless him (her) saying the following):* In the name of the Father of the Son and the Holy Spirit. Amen.

78. Prayer of a mother for a child with mental disabilities

Lord Jesus, Good and Merciful God, I thank You for this son (daughter) of mine that You have given me. Thank You for the gift of his (her) life, for his (her) innocence and for the great opportunity of sanctification You offer me through his (her) existence.

You have allowed **N/.** to be born with this condition, for this reason, it will not be possible for him (her) to grow up like the other children, therefore he (she) will always depend on me in a special way. I know that this dependence, although it can be somehow mitigated with time, and through special education, will be in the end permanent. I am aware that living like this will not be easy and that many people, seeing my situation and that of my child, will look at it as a terrible tragedy, that perhaps it would have been prevented by not having allowed him (her) to be born since because for many, a life like this is not worth living. I do not believe that, Lord.

I firmly believe that every human soul has an infinite value in Your presence, regardless of health, mental or bodily handicap and independently of their abilities. My child has been created according to Your image and likeness and I have no doubt that, in Your wisdom, You have willed his (her) life and his (her) existence for which I will always be grateful to You.

I only ask You to keep me healthy in order to always be there for my child. Give me the strength to help him (her), the patience to walk by his (her) side, that I may never make him (her) feel useless nor that he (she) represents a burden to me. Procure me the finances, material, medical and psychological means to give him (her) a quality of life worthy of a human being, created after Your image and likeness and redeemed by Your Precious Blood.

IV Prayers in Particular Circumstances

Have mercy on me, Lord, do not abandon me or forsake my little one. May the Virgin Mary, Your Mother and mine, and Saint Joseph, her Holy Spouse, guide me and teach me to be the best mother I can be for **N/**. May his (her) guardian angel always guard him (her) and keep him (her) safe from harm ways and all evil. I thank You once again for making him (her) so innocent and for giving him (her) the great gift of being unable to offend You. From the bottom of my heart, dear Lord, I thank You for Your great love for me and for the life of my little one. Amen.

79. Prayer for finding a good wife

Lord God and Creator of all that exist, You formed man in Your own image and likeness, and from his own flesh You provided him with a companion so that he would glorify You and thus, populate the face of the earth (cf. Gen 1: 27-28). Look at me with compassion and listen to my humble prayer, which I address to You, to Whom nothing is hidden and who knows what is best for us (cf. Dn 12: 9).

Help me; I beseech You, to find a good woman; the one You have designated for me from all eternity. I ask You that she be gifted with goodness, capable of loving me sincerely, a woman that can become my best friend and my faithful companion, my confidant and a shoulder where I find comfort in the midst of the many trials of life. May she be an enemy of lies, a friend of modesty, in every respect a faithful daughter of Yours, loyal to the faith of the Church and deeply devoted to Your Blessed Mother.

Help me to be a faithful reflection of Your love for her to the point of being willing to sacrifice my own life for her in the same way You have done for Your Church, Your beloved spouse, from the wood of the cross (cf. Eph 5:25). May our love be driven not by passions and instincts, but by a sincere desire to do good to each other in this world and seek our mutual salvation. Help us to accept with deep joy the children that You want to give us and to educate them in Your love and in Your laws in order to be witnesses of You and Your faithfulness in the world.

Grant me the grace to find the one whom You already know and who may also be praying to find me. Lord Jesus, make our paths come together and see in each other the sign of Your will for us, I ask this in Your holy Name in which I have placed all my trust. Amen.

80. Prayer for finding a good husband

Lord Jesus, Good and Provident God, I thank You for my life, for being a woman and for the many blessings You have given me throughout my life.

IV Prayers in Particular Circumstances

Good Lord, in Your divine will my future is hidden, a promising future that You have prepared for me even before I was born. I confess before Your majesty that it is my firm intention to discover it and to shape my life according to it because I know that in Your will, I shall find true happiness.

Through discernment and prayer, I feel that You are calling me to the sacrament of marriage, to start a family and thus serve You in this world. So, humbly, I want to ask You to help me to be attentive to Your signs, to find the man that Your providence already knows and with whom I can love You and serve You until the end of our lives.

Make our paths come together, that a sincere, pure, honest and true love may be born for one another. That he may be a man for whom You are his first priority and whose goal in life is seeking always to do Your will in all circumstances. May he be a righteous man who can help me to know You more and to always walk in holiness. A man who can challenge me in becoming a better person and who is also willing to be, himself, better every day. That he may be a man in whom I can entrust my heart, my life and my future, that completes me and with whom I may be happy. May he be a hardworking man, who could be a good father for our children, provident and determined to be faithful to me, as I will be to him. That he may be an enemy of vices, free of any addiction and any trauma that makes him unable to marry.

Prepare my heart so that I can also be for him a true companion, humble, respectful, truthful, in whom he can always find support in difficult times. May our love be fruitful and may we receive generously the children that You want to give us so we can educate them in the true faith to love and respect You always. May we both form an unbreakable unity in Your love, in order to resist the different blows and temptations that we will find in our path.

Help me to find a man with whom I can grow old with joy and peace. May we see our children's children and one day, together, contemplate the beauty of Your face in the kingdom of Your eternal love. Help me to find him, Lord, at the time and place where Your holy will so disposes. Amen.

81. Prayer of those who are engaged

Lord Jesus, beloved Father, today we come before You to plead for our love. Your loving providence allowed us to meet. Now we have decided to make a commitment, to get to know each other better in the hope that, in the near future, we can, with Your blessing, get married and start a new family in Your name.

That is why we have come to beg You with deep humility, let us discover if it is in Your will, that we remain together. That through fervent prayer, You may communicate to us Your will and by gazing on Your holy face, we may know in our hearts if we belong together.

IV Prayers in Particular Circumstances

Give us the gift of chastity to respect our bodies as sanctuaries of Your Spirit and never offend You with acts or thoughts of impurity. May we both live in perfect chastity until the day of our marriage in which You will join us to become one flesh.

Help us to not depart from You, so one day this love which we have for each other, and that for now is only human love may deserve to be transformed, by the grace of marriage, into Your love, divine love, indestructible love, infinite love, true and lasting love. Amen.

82. Prayer of a married couple

God of infinite love, with deep humility we place ourselves under Your inexhaustible mercy, and humbly ask You to bless our union. We are aware of our deep fragility and that without You our love could not be truthful.

You know well that our union does not respond only to purely human or carnal desires, but, inspired by Your Word, it was always our intention to establish a family founded on Your name and on Your mandates.

Our main goal is, therefore, to help each other, and between the two of us help our children, to achieve the eternal salvation that You have earned us with Your cross.

Protect us from division, pride, disordered passions, envy, indifference, selfishness, disaffection, resentment, desire for dominion and power and everything that undermines the foundations of true love.

You are, kind Lord, the principal guest of our home; do not ever leave us, and since only You are Good, it is only united with You that we can be good. You are, dear Lord, the rock and the guide of our lives, Your will is, beloved God, and not ours, the universal rule that governs our journey together.

Above all, rekindle everyday Your grace in our hearts, the same grace which we received at our wedding and which made us one flesh. Revive in us the gift of faithfulness and chastity, so we may love each other deeply in this world and through this love, be faithful witnesses of Yours before all men. Amen.

83. Prayer of a married couple in crisis

Lord Jesus, our teacher and our brother, we bless You and trust You. We thank You for all the good You have done for us, *(if there are children the following is said:* as well as for our children). You were the One who made our paths to come together, the One who inspired us to dream of sharing a future and a family. It was in Your power and in Your love that we were finally joined in marriage with the commitment of sharing our lives until death set us apart.

IV Prayers in Particular Circumstances

But now, Good and Merciful God, we experience the burden of our own limitations and fear that our marriage could collapse. That is why we come before You with deep humility to be healed by Your hand, the same hand that brough us together. The years, the routine, our failures and so many problems have weakened our love. We do not ignore though that this love that unites us is no longer only human but also divine.

Indeed, on the day of our wedding, we promised to be faithful in the prosperous and adverse times, in health and in sickness and to love and respect each other every day of our lives (cf. Rite of Marriage). Upon receiving our vows, You covered our limited and small human love with the greatness of Your divine, infinite and eternal love. That is why we know that within us, in our union, You have deposited all the graces we need to come out victorious from this storm that has broken out over our marriage.

Come to our lives, forgive our sins and help us forgive each other. Heal our wounds, erase all resentment, expel all pride, renew our faith, awake our hope and fill us with charity toward one another. Help us, Lord, to be always mindful that we are no longer two, but one flesh in You (cf. Mt 19: 6). Take away from us the cancer of selfishness, indifference, coldness and divorce which, Lord, we know You detest (cf. Ml 2:16). Help us to fight for our marriage, for our family (and for our children). In Your holy love we trust, Lord, have mercy on us and rekindle our love with Yours. Holy Mary and Saint Joseph, Saint Priscilla, Saint Monica and Saint Thomas More pray for us. Amen.

84. Prayer of divorced and remarried

Lord Jesus, God of infinite mercy, I thank You for so many good things that You have done for me throughout my life. *(if there are children the following is said:* I especially thank You for all my children; they are all wonderful gifts from Your hand). Today I humbly ask You to kindly incline Your ear towards me and listen to my poor and humble prayer. It is true, I have departed from You, but now I want to return home.

The difficulties in my life, my bad decisions, perhaps also my ignorance of Your laws, and my fears of being alone led me to start a relationship with a woman (man) outside the sanctity of marriage. You have told us *"that is why man will leave his father and mother, and they will both become one flesh. So, there are no longer two, but only one flesh. Therefore, what God has united man should not separate"* (Mk 10: 7-9). I am still united to a marriage that unfortunately did not work and according to Your law, I should not cohabitate with the woman (man) with whom I am presently living.

In this situation, although I know that I can attend holy Mass and for this I sincerely thank You, I am unable to receive the absolution of my sins and consequently receive Holy Communion. This is a cause of a deep pain for me, since You have said that whoever does not eat Your Body and does not drink Your Blood cannot have eternal life (cf. Jn 6: 51-58). From the depths of my darkness, I come to You, Good Lord, so that, giving light to my eyes and dispelling the darkness of my mind, I might

IV Prayers in Particular Circumstances

clearly see what Your holy Church teaches and what You expect of me. And once I can understand what You want, give me the strength and courage to put into practice and without delay Your holy will.

You are my true Shepherd, Lord, help me to hear Your voice and differentiate it from those voices that, driven by false compassion and mercy, try to convince me that it is possible to participate in the Eucharistic banquet in my current condition. I, who want to live in the truth, know that this is not true.

My Sweet Lord Jesus, I humbly beg You not to abandon me to my circumstances, but to help me recover Your grace soon so, I may receive You again in Holy Communion. You know that I love the woman (the man) with whom I live, *(if there are children...* and that with her (him) I have already formed a family). But I know well that without You, it is impossible to be happy. Help me, I beseech You, to discern soon, by the hand of Your Church, if my first marriage was valid. If so, help me to regularize my situation so I can marry the woman (the man) with whom I now live and thus, return to the sacraments and to Your friendship.

In the event that the Church sanctioned that my first marriage is still valid, and therefore, it is impossible for me to marry the woman (the man) whom I live now, I beg You, Good Lord, to give us both the gift of perfect chastity to be able to live no longer as husband and wife, but as brother and sister. In this way, keeping the unity of our home, we can also please You, and with Your grace participate in fullness of the salvation You offer us.

I am so happy to know that You, Lord, leave the ninety-nine sheep to go in search of the lost one and that there is more joy in heaven for a sinner who repents than for ninety-nine righteous people who do not need to convert (cf. Lc 15, 7: 14). Look at me, then, with compassion. Do not forget me. Come and rescue me from this situation. Good Shepherd, gently carry me on Your shoulders and take me back to Your flock. Amen.

85. Prayer of a pregnant woman

Lord Jesus, God of life and innocence, I thank You for the gift of fertility and for allowing me to conceive this new life in my womb. This life is still small, fragile and imperceptible to the human eye, but it is the life of a human being, with all the dignity that is given to him (her) to have been made after Your own image and likeness. In Your infinite love, You have created the soul of my baby and now inside me, You have started to form his (her) body, make him (her) grow with health and normality. Deliver him (her), I beg You, from all malformation and from all disease.

Through this prayer I also want to consecrate my baby to You. In shaping his (her) mind, make it in a way that he (she) may always use it to know You and jealously guard the light of the true faith; in shaping his (her) eyes, do it so he (she) can always see clearly to never walk straight from You. By forming his mouth and his tongue, fashion it in a way that he (she) may always proclaim Your praises; When forming his (her) ears, endow them with the ability to always be attentive to listen to Your Word and obey it without delay. When forming his (her) little feet, make them in a way that he (she) may always walk along Your paths; by forming his little hands make them in a way that he (she) may use them to tireless build Your kingdom in this world.

And finally, when forming his (her) heart, forge it in such a way that he (she) never closes it to Your inspirations, but, on the contrary, may use it to always love You above all and may this heart remain restless until it finds rest in You (cf. St. Augustine, Confessions). Grant him (her) the joy that, as soon as possible, once born to this world, he (she) may receive the grace of baptism and thus, be freed from the power of the evil one and transformed from a simple creature into a child of Yours.

To me, Your servant, give me good health, deliver me from any accident and allow me to carry this pregnancy to term that, in Your goodness You have granted me to have. You, Who in Your wisdom wanted to enter this world through the pure bosom of Your most holy Mother; do not turn Your loving presence away from my baby. Remain with him (her) throughout his (her) life in such a way that both of us may enjoy together one day the eternal glory of Your kingdom. Amen.

86. Prayer asking for fertility

Lord and God of all that exists, at the end of Your creation and as the culmination of it, You made man and woman and gave them the command to be fruitful and multiply in order to populate the face of the earth (cf. Gen 1:28).

Throughout the history of salvation, in Your infinite mercy, You did not despise the prayers of those women who, having been denied the possibility of having children naturally, humbly implored of You, the gift of fertility. Thus, from the beginning of Your revelation, faithful to the promise You made to Abraham, You made fertile the barren womb of Sarah, his wife, who conceived Isaac in her old age (cf. Gen 21: 1). From Isaac You also heard his prayer and gave Rebekah, his wife, unable to have children, the joy of conceiving Jacob (cf. 25: 21) in whom You would fulfill Your promise to Abraham to give him a more numerous offspring than the stars of the sky and the sands of the seashore (cf. 15: 5).

You granted Leah and Rachel a similar favor, through which, despite their infertility, You gave children to Jacob, thus increasing Your holy people (cf. 29: 31; 30: 22). The same happened with Manoah's wife (cf. Jgs13: 2-3) whom in Your mercy You heard, giving him an offspring, and with Ana wife of Elcana whose prayer was pleasing to You and to whom You granted to give birth to Your servant Samuel (cf. 1 Sam 1: 17-20; 27-28).

Finally, in the dawn of salvation You heard the prayer of Elizabeth, wife of Zechariah, who had reached her old age without conceiving a child. She became the mother of the forerunner of Your beloved Son, the one who would prepare his way (cf. Lk 1: 3).

In this way, and because of Your great kindness and compassion, all these women whose wombs were not able to conceive, could shout for joy when they saw that

IV Prayers in Particular Circumstances

more were the children of the desolate woman than of her who had a husband (cf. Is 54: 1; Gal 4:27).

Hence, Lord God of mercy, You who open and close the womb of Your daughters (cf. Is 66: 9) and for Whom nothing at all is impossible (cf. Lk 1:37) I come to You, with the same confidence with which all these women raised their prayers, to beg You, with deep humility, to grant me the grace to conceive a child and bring him (her) successfully to birth.

Heal my womb; sprinkle it with the power of Your Spirit, the same Spirit that flew over the oceans when You created the heavens and the earth (cf. Gen 1: 1-2). Give my womb the fecundity You gave to the earth at the beginning of creation, so that I may embrace a child of my own. If You grant me this great favor that I ask with deep humility and faith, I will consecrate him (her) to You in a special way. Look, Lord, at my suffering and grant me what I ask of You so that my child and I may, after a life full of joy and holiness, praise You for all eternity in Your kingdom of infinite glory. Amen.

87. Prayer of a widow

Lord Jesus, Good and Gracious God, I direct my prayer to You with deep humility. I am a widow who, with great confidence, asks for Your protection and providence. I am inspired by knowing about Your predilection and favor for widows who suffer injustice and abandonment. Already in the Old Testament, Your Holy Father, made it very clear that, in his eyes, abusing widows and orphans was a great crime, so He established as a priority for His people to take care of them at all times (cf. Deut 6:18).

The gospels teach that like Your Father, You were also touched by the suffering and precarious situation of the widows of Your time (cf. Lk 7: 11-15). Indeed, Lord, it was a widow whose name was Anna, who in the Temple awaited You with confidence and hope. Once she looked at You with her own eyes, she dedicated the rest of her life to speak of Your coming to all who came to the temple (cf. Lc 2: 36-38). Later in Your mission, You were pleased by a widow's generosity, who gave everything she had as an offering in the temple (cf. Mk 12: 41-44) and it was also the persistence of a widow in her pursuit to obtain justice, which You set as an example to encourage those who listened to You to pray without ceasing (cf. Lk 18: 1-5).

Finally, You expressed Your displeasure on different occasions when the powerful took advantage of them and their possessions (cf. Mk 12: 38-40). That is why Your Church, from its very beginnings strived to follow Your example to meet the needs of all widows (cf. Acts 6: 1).

Hence, Good Lord, because of this predilection that You have shown towards the widows of the Bible, I - a widow like them – have felt encouraged to come to You with great confidence, knowing that my petitions will not be left unattended.

Listen, then, to my humble prayer. I pray especially for the soul of my late husband **N/**. Forgive his sins and lead him to the joy of Your glory. Bless my

IV Prayers in Particular Circumstances

children and my grandchildren; always accompany them, free them from all evil and do not let them stray away from You. Comfort me, Lord, in my solitude; provide me with what I need to live with dignity and honestly. I offer myself to You and everything that I am and have so the message of Your Gospel can be spread. May all who see me see in me a clear sign of Your love and Your faithfulness to those who hope in You. And when the time to leave this world comes give me the grace of a holy death so I may deserve to behold forever the beauty of Your face. I praise You and bless You, Lord; You alone are enough for me. Amen.

88. Prayer of a boy

Jesus, dear friend, You have told through Your Gospel that You like to be around children, to listen and to talk to them. Thank You for Your love and Your friendship, thank You for suffering and for dying for me. Please, take care of my Dad and my Mom. I ask You to always provide work for him (them). Take care of my brother(s) and sister(s) as well and help me not to fight with them but on the contrary to love them very much and always be good to them. Let there be peace in the whole world and grant that no child be hungry today or stop smiling.

You know, Lord, how much I want to grow up and become strong. Help me to behave well with my parents and also at school. Forgive me because sometimes I am selfish and arrogant and for not being willing to share my things with others. Jesus, I ask You also that even when I grow up and learn new things, may I never stop being Your friend. Dear Jesus, You are so Good and

Awesome; I thank You for that. Please stay always with me and make me holy. Amen.

89. Prayer of an altar boy

Jesus, dear friend, You are so Good with me and with the whole world. You love children and You always want to be with them. I thank You for calling me to serve You at Your altar as Your servant. Help me to always show in Your house, the church, all the reverence, respect and adoration of which I am capable. May I always behave well and help my peers at the altar to do the same.

I firmly believe that in the holy Mass, You become truly present in Your Body and in Your Blood, in Your Soul and in Your Divinity to save me and the world. That is why I am very happy to know that I am close to You at this great moment in the company of the Virgin Mary, my Mother.

I give You my life - my present and my future- and I want You to know that I will always be attentive to Your voice, ready to listen to whatever You want to tell me. Show me the right way to live my life according to Your will and thus, serve You better. You are so good and kind dear Jesus, once again I thank You for everything. Please stay always with me and make me holy! Amen.

IV Prayers in Particular Circumstances

90. Prayer of a quinceañera (fifteen birthday)

Lord Jesus, my Father and my Lord, I come before Your altar today to thank You for my life and for my fifteen years.

Thank You for my parents, my relatives and my friends who have come to join me today. I ask that on this day You grant me the graces that I need at this time of my life to become a good woman, a worthy daughter of Yours and an example for my friends. That is why I come before You with humility, but with joy to beg You to grant me many virtues and graces.

Today I want to express exteriorly what I hope always to be interiorly. This beautiful dress and the way I have arranged myself is all for You. They want to express the beauty with which You have created my soul which I hope I have kept clean, pure and beautiful before Your eyes.

Especially today I ask You for the virtue of purity that is guarded with that of modesty. Teach me, then, to respect the sanctity of my body, in the way I dress, in the way I speak and in the way that I conduct myself among my friends. That in everything I do I may behave as Your faithful servant and not as a daughter of this passing world. Give me prudence and good judgment to faithfully and jealously guard my virginity and thus prepare to serve You whether You call me to marriage or to a consecrated life.

I also ask You for the gift of obedience. Now I am not a little girl anymore but a young lady; however, I am still under my parents' authority for which I owe them obedience and respect. Help me, then, that just like You, I also be obedient to those who seek the best for me and continue to grow in wisdom, stature and grace (cf. Lk 2:52).

Listen to me, Lord, on this my special day. Do not let my youthfulness become my hindrance to staying near You. During this time, help me to live closer to You and grow in my faith. May what Your beloved disciple said about overcoming the evil one be fulfilled in me (cf 1 Jn 2:13). I invoke the protection of Your Blessed Mother, whom I consecrate myself to - body and soul -. Amen.

91. Prayer for perfect chastity

Lord Jesus, true God and true Man, and as a chaste and pure Man, totally consecrated to the fulfillment of the will of Your Father, before You I prostrate myself with deep humility to ask You for the precious gift of perfect chastity.

In Your infinite wisdom, You have chosen some of Your children so that, by renouncing marriage and the mutual gift of conjugal life, they can witness in their own flesh and in a tangible way the realities of the future life (cf. Mt 19: 12) and devote themselves completely to the service of Your Gospel.

This is a holy and sublime vocation to which You have been pleased to call me. Thus, with this vocation, You enrich Your Church and manifest in a living way that

IV Prayers in Particular Circumstances

You did not create us for any creature, but only for You, in Whom every man and woman find their true fulfillment.

That is why today I come before You to implore You with confidence that, since You have called me to this sublime vocation, without any merit on my part, You may grant me to live it out fully. You know, Lord, that although I have been called to this vocation, I am not free from the whirlwind of my passions and the insidious sting of the flesh. As the Apostle, I have asked You many times to set me free from it, and like him You have answered: *"My grace is enough for you"* (cf. 2 Cor 12: 9). Have mercy on me, O Lord!

Confident that You will grant me this grace I solemnly profess - once again - that it is my will and my free determination, to follow You in perfect chastity. Thus, I humbly ask You, Lord, to guard my eyes from every immodest image. Make me keep my ears away from every seductive word. Place a seal on my lips to avoid any impure conversation. Make me free from any attachments to friendships that do not have You as the center. May my dealings with women (men) always be marked by respect and prudence. May I see them as what they really are, daughters (sons) of Yours and temples of Your Holy Spirit, and never as objects of my pleasure.

May I, through a deep prayer life, develop a solid friendship with You that makes me despise this world with all its empty promises, so that, free of all earthly ties, I may be able to give myself totally to Your service and that of my brothers and sisters and so to deserve, one day, the joyful contemplation of the incomparable beauty of

Your face. My Lord and my God, You are the only love of my soul, *"You are part of my inheritance and my cup, You hold my lot"* (Ps 16: 5). Amen.

92. Prayer asking for discernment

Lord, You have willed to make known to us Your holy will from the beginning of creation, so that man, who already carries Your law in his conscience, can follow You and live in peace.

Indeed, Your will is not really far from us up in heaven for us to say: *"Who will ascend into heaven to get it and proclaim it to us so we may obey it? Nor is it beyond the sea, so that you have to ask, 'Who will cross the sea to get it and proclaim it to us so we may obey it?' No,* -As You have said- *the word is very near you; it is in your mouth and in your heart so you may obey it"* (cf. Dt. 30: 12-14). Indeed, You have not talked to us in secret, nor have You asked us to seek You in vain (cf. Is 45: 19).

However, sin and our exile away from Your face causes us many times to not see clearly what You expect of us. That is why I (we) ask Your forgiveness, and I (we) beg You with deep humility, to enlighten my (our) mind (minds) to be able to be filled with the knowledge of Your will in all wisdom and spiritual understanding (cf. Col 1: 9, 4, 2), and thus, to be able to know and clearly see Your will in my (our) life (lives). *"Speak, Lord, that Your servant listens"* (1 Sm 3:

IV Prayers in Particular Circumstances

10), let me (us) know what I (we) should do in this specific situation *(mention the situation in which one wants to know God's will)*. Help me (us) to discover what You want from me (us). Give me (us) clarity and courage to put it diligently and effectively into practice in such a way, that You can always find in me (us) Your most faithful servant(s) and hence my (our) life (lives) may be always pleasing before Your eyes. I (We) ask this through Christ our Lord. Amen.

93. Prayer for discerning a vocation

God, Father of mercies, I thank You for everything You have done for me: for giving me my life, my parents, my faith and always being with me when I needed You most.

Today I come before Your presence to ask You for discernment, to know what Your divine will has prepared for me. I know, Lord, that You created me for You and I know that nothing in the world will give me the happiness that only being obedient to Your will can give me. I also know that You have not left me adrift in this world, but that You have placed Your law in my heart as a guide for my journey. Finally, You have sent Your Son as a true man to talk to me through the Gospel in a way I can understand, with the sole purpose to show me the path that will lead me to my salvation.

But now in the dawn of my youth, I come before You to ask for Your assistance in order to discern which vocation You are calling me to; *"Speak, Lord that Your servant listens"* (1 S 3: 10). Let me know Your will. I promise You that once I learn it, I will not go away as the young man of the Gospel did (cf. Mt 19:22), but that I will put all the means to carry it out and follow You in any state of life that You may well call me. Whether in marriage or in consecrated life, let me know what Your divine wisdom has prepared for me.

Make me attentive to Your inspirations, open to Your motions, let me identify Your signs and recognize Your voice. I belong to Your flock, Lord, I am one of Your sheep, I know that You know me and that I will not perish by Your side, nor will I be taken from Your hand (cf. Jn 17:28). I want to follow You wherever You call me without delay, without excuses and without looking back (cf. Lk 9: 57-62).

Most importantly, Good Lord, in any way You decide to call me, give me the grace to persevere in it. Do not let me stray from You, nor deviate me from Your path, nor get lost by following the deceptive compass of my own will. Dear Jesus, I am firmly convinced that life is not life if I do not live it according to Your divine will. Thus, once again: *"Speak, Lord, that Your servant listens"* (1 S 3: 10). Amen.

94. Prayer of a pastor or chaplain

Lord, Good Shepherd, eternal priest, unique and true Mediator between God and men, I thank You infinitely for giving me the ineffable gift of the priesthood. You, Lord, without any merit on my part, have deigned to

IV Prayers in Particular Circumstances

call me as shepherd of this portion of Your holy people to administer Your sacraments and to preach Your Word.

I humbly ask You for this community that You have entrusted to me. Without You I am only able to spoil Your redemptive work. My talents and my gifts are nothing without Your grace and Your assistance. Therefore, in order to succeed in this mission You have entrusted me, humbly, I ask You to grant me the following three gifts.

First, make my lips and my tongue burn in the desire to preach with integrity Your word as the prophets, apostles and martyrs once did. May I be faithful to Your Gospel which You have entrusted to Your Church, which - under the action of the Holy Spirit in its dogmas and teachings - has faithfully transmitted its true meaning throughout the centuries.

Second, light my heart with the fervent desire for holiness so that I can witness before Your people, not only in word, but also in my life that it is possible to live according to Your commandments and thus, find happiness. Make me a penitent man, and a man of deep prayer for my people. Deliver me from mediocrity, tepidity and a double life.

Finally, oh sweet Shepherd, create in me with the fire of Your Spirit a shepherd's heart, not according to my will, or according to human standards, but according to Your heart (cf. Jer 3:15). That I may always share the joy of Your Gospel, show mercy to the sinner, have patience with those who err, give the best advice to the confused, and be prudent and wise in the way I present to everyone Your message of salvation.

Give me, therefore, Lord, the wisdom to live my priesthood enriched with these three gifts. May they free me from seeking recognition, engaging in careerism and making my priority something other than the salvation of the souls entrusted to my care. But above all, Lord, never let me give up in my race toward my own salvation, *"... lest after preaching to others I myself should be disqualified."* (1 Cor 9: 27). Amen.

95. Prayer of the catechumens

Lord Jesus, my Master and my Savior, I thank You for calling me from the darkness of sin to Your admirable light (cf. 1 Pt 2: 9; Col 1:13). In recent months I have been preparing myself in order to know You better. Your history with humanity since the beginning of creation has deeply touched me. It has amazed me how You formed Your people Israel from an old man (cf. Gen 12: 1-3) and patiently led him through generations until You gave him Your Law on mount Sinai (cf. Ex 20: 1-21). Since that day, through the voice of the prophets, You persistently called him to return to You every time he departed from Your Covenant (cf. 2 Cor 7: 14. 30, 9b; Jl 2: 13; Is 44: 22).

It has filled me with joy and awe to know how in the fullness of time You came to meet us (cf. Ga 4:4) and offered Yourself for all men on the cross from which Your Church was born (cf. Jn 19: 34). In this Church, You have deposited unfathomable goods and riches offered to all those who believe that You are the Lord and who have confessed Your victory over death and sin (cf. Rom 10:

IV Prayers in Particular Circumstances

9). All this has strengthened my faith in You and made me reaffirm my conviction that You are the Christ, the Son of the living God who has to come into the world (cf. Jn 11:27; Mt 16:16).

All the benefits of this saving history will be present in me in the context of the Easter Vigil. There I will be baptized -"plunged" into the water that symbolizes my burial into Christ's death- from which I will rise up by resurrecting with him as "a new creature" (cf. CCC # 1214; Rom 6: 3-4; Col 2: 12; Ti 3: 5). In this way, I will go from being a simple creature created by Your hand to a child of Yours (cf. 1 Jn 3: 1), member of Your Church (cf. 1 Col 12: 3; 1 Pt 2, 5) and heir of the life to come (cf. Jn 3:36). All of this, O Lord, will take place in me on that glorious night of Easter for which my heart is filled with joy and forever I will sing Your praises (cf. Ps 145: 21).

At the same time, Lord of incomparable glory, I will receive the sacrament of confirmation. This sacrament is the fullness of the gift of the Holy Spirit which will be imposed on me as a holy anointing, which will make me a militant Christian and an adult in the faith. I will be marked by the Spirit with its indelible seal that will make me Your property (cf. 2 Cor 1:21; Eph 4:30).

Finally, Lord Jesus, once I have been made a new creature, I will be able to approach Your altar to be fed by You with Your Body and with Your Blood, food of eternal life (cf. Jn 6:51) and pledge of the glory to come (cf. CCC # 1402).

That holy night I will be initiated into all these mysteries that will transform me into a full Christian (cf.

Eph 4: 7), endowed with all the necessary graces to live a new life in perfect holiness (cf. 2 Cor 5:17). After this, You will send me to the world as Your apostle in order to spread Your Word among my brothers and sisters and, with Your help, win them over for You (cf. Mk 16:15-16).

I beseech You, Good Lord, that once I embrace You by professing this Catholic faith, I may never suffer the misery of departing from You by abandoning the true faith. Help me, I beg, You to always treasure it and defend it even with my own life.

Lord, until today I have lived in ignorance of You under the power of sin and death but now, I freely want to leave behind the idols and everything regarding my past life that opposed Your will and greatly offended You. I declare that I want to become Your disciple for pure love of You because life without You is not worth living. Amen.

96. Prayer of the extraordinary ministers of Holy Communion

Lord Jesus, Good and Provident God, I thank You for giving me the gift of baptism and making me a partaker in Your priesthood in the common order of the faithful.

In the midst of this crisis of priestly vocations, You wanted to call me to collaborate in this extraordinary ministry by distributing Your most holy Body and Your most precious Blood to my brothers and sisters.

IV Prayers in Particular Circumstances

Increase my faith so that I can undoubtedly believe everything that the Church teaches about Your real presence in the holy Host and in the sacred Chalice. Make me more generous with the time I spend in prayer in front the Blessed Sacrament and through this beautiful act of piety, make me more deeply aware of the nature of this great mystery which, despise my unworthiness, You have called me to serve as an extraordinary minister. Grant me, Lord, to never spare any respect, cleanliness, adoration or gentleness before Your sacred presence in the most holy Eucharist.

That at all times, I may demonstrate through my bodily gestures my deep faith in You, Whom I will hold in my hands. But above all, Lord, I ask You to increase the number of holy and well-formed priests and deacons throughout the world, so that the distribution of this great Sacrament may be administered only by those who have directly and ordinarily received from You the commission of this sacred ministry. Amen.

97. Prayer of the ministers of music during the Holy Mass

Lord Jesus, God of perfection and harmony, You are absolute Beauty and in You there is nothing imperfect or mediocre. In Your great goodness, You have called us to this ministry of music, to help the glory of the Holy Mass be more clearly appreciated by Your holy people. That is why we ask You to assist us with Your Spirit, so that in our service we will always be pleasing to Your majesty.

"Lord, I love the house where You live, the place where Your glory dwells" (Ps 26: 8) there, the incomparable mystery of the Holy Mass is present. In this holy Sacrifice, O Lord of Beauty, *"... You are very great; You are clothed with splendor and majesty, You wrap Yourself in light as with a garment"* (Ps 104: 1). That is why we can say, without any doubt, that the Eucharist is the most beautiful and sacred action that exists on this side of heaven. Having been invited to it to serve You with our voices and instruments constitutes a very high privilege which is the cause of a great joy. At the same time, we feel a great responsibility to do it well since our music will join that of the angelic choirs that in heaven sing Your glory.

We know that the Holy Mass is Your holy Sacrifice. It is not our work; it does not depend on our ideas or our improvisations. Therefore, deliver us, O Lord, from using it to stand out or draw attention to us: *"Not to us, Lord, not to us, but to Your name give glory"* (Ps 115: 1). With deep humility, we beg You not to allow us to fall into mediocrity, conformity, ignorance and pride by believing that we know everything. May we always be willing to learn and give You the best of ourselves. Help us understand that goodwill is not enough and that talent, knowledge, quality, effort and discipline are also necessary.

Assist us, Lord, with Your Spirit and deliver us from subjectivity and relativism so our service may be based on an appreciation of objective beauty. That, at all times, we may be truly aware of the true spirit of the liturgy and its deep meaning. May we value and teach others to appreciate the musical tradition of Your Church in the

IV Prayers in Particular Circumstances

style and in the way in which, throughout the centuries, You inspired her to sing Your holy mysteries. Do not allow our music to fall into superficiality of the fashions and rhythms of this world, but on the contrary, imbued by the perennial mystery of Your glory; may it elevate the minds and the hearts of Your people – by the beauty of sacred music - to the eternal realities where You invite Your people to partake in each Eucharist. Amen.

98. Prayer of an artist

Lord and God of all beauty, with deep humility I approach You to thank You for giving me the gift of art and thus able to proclaim Your greatness and Your perfection among men.

I praise You and thank You concretely for the gift of *(mentioning the art in which You have talent: music, singing, painting, etc.)* ... Through it, You allow me to bring comfort, hope and light to a world many times submerged in ugliness, chaos and superficiality caused by sin and death.

I also beg Your pardon because many times I have not used as I should these gifts that You so generously have given me. Forgive me for having sought my own glory and not Yours. And finally, for the times in which I have been arrogant and proud thinking that it is in me and not in You where the source of my gifts originates.

Deliver me, I beseech You, Lord, from vanity and a dissolute life, which obfuscate the human heart misleading it into perdition. Thus, assist me, Good God, to cultivate my gifts to become the best *(singer, musician, painter, etc.)* I can be in order to more and more resemble You Who are absolute perfection. May the beauty that I express through my art be true and transcendent. May I never use the gift You have given me to serve the world and his prince, the father of lies (cf. Jn 8:44); deliver me from the temptation of sacrificing everything, even my soul, before the altar of fame and money. Assist me, rather, so that through my talents I may help men to raise their minds and their hearts from this passing world to the supernatural and eternal realities that lead to You.

Do not allow, Lord, that I be seduced by a false, empty and deceptive beauty behind which the prince of this world hides himself dressed as an angel of light, seeking to turn us away from You. O Beauty always old and ever new, since You have given me the grace of reflecting Your radiance through my art, give me also, I beseech You, through my life to better express the great goodness that comes from You.

Finally, I humbly ask You that, since in this life I have endeavored to reflect through my skills the beauty of Your face, once I finish the trajectory of my mortal life may I fully contemplate You face to face in the infinite glory of Your kingdom where You are so great and Your garments are splendor and majesty (cf. Ps 104: 1). Amen.

99. Prayer of a fallen away catholic

Lord Jesus, loving Father, have mercy on me, a poor sinner. With all my heart I thank You for the gift of faith that I received from my parents. When I was little,

IV Prayers in Particular Circumstances

they brought me to Your house so I could be born again through baptism which gave me eternal life. This was a gift that infinitely exceeded the gift my parents gave me of bringing me into this life. In that baptismal font, I went from being a creature of Yours to being Your child and heir of Your eternal glory. I thank You also for the gift of my confirmation through which, in Your goodness, I became Your soldier. Finally, I will never forget that glorious day of my first communion in which, as innocent child, I received Your Body and Your Blood for the first time.

But, Lord, it happened with me as with that seed of the parable of the Gospel, which fell along the road, Your Word reached my ears, but I did not understand it, the devil came and snatched it from my heart. Or perhaps as with the seed that was sown in stony rocks, for a moment I received Your Word with joy, but it didn't take root in me, and when the affliction came, I abandoned You. Or perhaps rather, it was like that seed that fell among thorns and was drowned by the evils of this time and the deception of wealth and ended up dying (cf. Mk 4:13-20; Lk 8:11-15).

But I know that it is not too late to re-sow the seed of my faith so it now can finally fall on fertile ground. Yes, Lord, the shortcomings and miseries of my life have fertilized the land of my existence and now I am ready to receive Your seed and bear much fruit. That is why I raise my humble prayer to You Whom I know leave the ninety-nine sheep to go in search of the one that is lost (cf. Lk 15: 3). Look at me with extreme mercy, carry me on Your shoulders and take me back to Your Church from which I should never have moved away.

Help me to be a good Catholic, to discover in the Holy Mass the source and the climax of my life. Never, Lord, never again, may I neglect the Sunday precept because without receiving Your Body and Your Blood I cannot have eternal life in me (cf. Jn 6:58). As of today, I will seek frequent sacramental confession and if it happened that in my life there is a situation that prevent me from receiving these sacraments, show me the way back. I beg You not to abandon me to my circumstances. I have understood that mortal sin kills my soul and deprives me of Your grace, without which there can be no salvation. May I faithfully fulfill all Your commandments. May I always be willing to forgive those who have hurt me and also may I have the humility to ask forgiveness from those whom I have offended.

Give me Your grace, Lord, to cultivate a deep life of prayer that will help me to persevere in my Christian life to which, full of joy, I return today. Change my lukewarm heart for one on fire with love for You. And finally, grant me a deep devotion to Your Blessed Mother through the daily recitation of the Holy Rosary and never again, Lord of infinite mercy, never again let me stray from You and from

IV Prayers in Particular Circumstances

the bosom of my mother the holy Catholic Church. Amen.

100. Prayer asking for love of God

Lord God of mercy, You are a God of infinite love. I humbly ask You to look at me with compassion and infuse into my soul the purest love for Your Divine Majesty. Only in loving You above all things can true happiness be found. Therefore, I give You my heart I pray that You may never find in it, the smallest corner where You are not perfectly loved.

Do not let me give to any creature the same love that, as my Creator and Redeemer, only You deserve. May You always be my main priority, and the primary focus of my thoughts and my will. In short, I fervently desire for You to be at the center of my whole being.

May I love You to such an extent, Lord, that my mortal life becomes impossible to be lived apart from You, so that death may be for me the sweetest liberation of the chains of this world, and my entry into Your kingdom, the ultimate realization of my entire existence. Amen.

101. Prayer before driving

Lord Jesus, Way, Truth and Life (cf. Jn 14: 6), I ask You at the beginning of this trip to accompany me and guide me on my journey. Give firmness to my hands, light and clarity to my eyes, complete dominion of all my senses to be able to drive in such a way that I may reach my destination looking after my own safety, as well as the safety of those who travel with me. Lord, deliver me from the terrible tragedy that by some carelessness of mine, I may cause harm to someone.

Finally, help me to run with perseverance the race that You have marked out for me, fixing my eyes on Jesus, the pioneer and perfecter of faith (cf. Heb 12: 1). Never allow me to leave Your path, however narrow and difficult it may be, because I am certain that persevering in it will lead me to enjoy one day the greatness of Your loving presence. Amen.

102. Prayer of the elderly

Lord of my parents and my youth, Good Companion of my long journey, I give You thanks for the life that You have given me, for all these years in which You have accompanied me both in my sorrows as in my joys. You have given me so many things that enumerating them would be simply impossible. For all of them I thank You and I praise You. Forgive me for the things that I could have done better but did not because of my sins.

Only You know my heart. Have mercy on me for my numerous failings. There is so much wisdom in Your Word: *"Vanity of vanities all is vanity"* (cf. Ecc 1:1) Now in my old age when the snows of time have covered my head, I come before You with humility since I have no more pride left. A lot of my friends and relatives with whom I

IV Prayers in Particular Circumstances

shared my childhood and my youth, have already left this world and gone before You: for their souls I ask forgiveness. I am being left alone and I am experiencing the burden, the limitations and the fragility of my age. Have mercy on me, O Lord!

That is why with great humility I come to You today, God of infinite Goodness, to ask You, above all, for patience to deal with this old and tired body. Help me to be thankful and kind with those who strive to help me and who with great love and sacrifice take care of me. Give me the magnanimity to forgive those to whom I gave so much, but now seem to have forgotten that I exist. I came from You, Lord, and I am going to You. *"Even when I am old and gray, do not forsake me, my God"* (cf. Ps 71: 18). Now that clarity sometimes leaves my mind, please never let Your grace leave my soul. Although weak and old I am still tempted and I can still suffer the misfortune of losing You. Do not allow it, Lord!

Good Father, accompany me in this last stage of my life. Look upon my loneliness and make me feel Your presence, look upon my sadness and make me rejoice with Your promises, look upon my weaknesses and strengthen my faith and look upon my suffering and purify me of my sins. I ask You also for my children and my grandchildren, let them not lose the faith that I passed on to them less they be separated from You.

Assist me to be prepared when death comes. Do not let me leave this earthly dwelling without Your sacramental help, and without having been reconciled with You and my brothers and sisters. Lord, finally, I beseech You to grant me the grace of a holy death in Your company, that of Our Lady and my father, Saint Joseph. Amen

103. Prayer of the physician

Lord Jesus, You are the Doctor of souls and bodies. In no one but You, mankind finds such a great, Good and Solicitous Benefactor. As the Good Samaritan You carry the wounded, bandage their wounds pouring the oil of truth and the wine of charity onto them. Then, through Your grace, You lead them to the Church where You care for them seeing to their full recovery (cf. Lk 10:34). I give You infinite thanks for giving me this wonderful vocation of caring for those who suffer under the yoke of disease, as well as ensuring that everyone is in good health.

In Your presence, O kind and holy Physician, I beg You to assist me with Your Spirit so that I may also be a Good Samaritan to all those whom I find wounded at the edge of life. Make my work be pleasing to You. May the sick find in me the same patience, the same respect and the same mercy they found in You during Your mortal life. Give life to my intelligence so that I might always find the right diagnosis. Open my ears so that I can carefully listen to the needs and pains of those who come to me for relief. Bless my hands so they can heal and relieve the pain and the suffering. Make me always attentive, O Lord, that I may not make a mistake that could harm those who put their lives and their health under my care.

Above all, Supreme and Sublime Doctor, I beg You that those who come to see me not only seek the healing of their bodies, but also that of their souls. May their lives be a constant search for Your will and, having found You in this world, may they one day enjoy Your kingdom forever: that glorious kingdom where there will be no more tears, no disease, no pain, no suffering, that blessed kingdom where death will never again have more power over us (cf. Rev 21: 4).

For me, Good Lord, I ask that You come to the help my soul and my body, that I may always work not for a sordid salary, but in order to fulfill the goal of my vocation which is to serve well those in need. Finally, I beg You to help me keep my job so I can continue to provide a decent life for my own family. Filled with confidence in Your protection and providence I place them under Your protection and care. Only in You does man find his fullness and his wholeness. Lord, mighty King, I beseech You, listen to this, my humble and poor prayer. Amen.

104. Prayer before a surgery

Lord Jesus, Sweet Doctor of soul and body, I humbly beg You to assist me with Your power and Your grace in this surgery which I am about to undergo. Give me, I humbly ask You, the peace of mind and spirit, and the confidence of knowing that I am in Your hands. Prepare everything in my body so this intervention may be a success.

Illumine the mind and the hands of the surgeons. Give them serenity, concentration and precision in their work so that they can satisfactorily fulfill the objective of this surgery. Assist everyone who will participate in my operation so they can do their jobs well.

May this surgery be the beginning of my healing process and the starting point of a fast recovery. By Your cross and resurrection, deliver me from any complications and sudden death. That once healthy and strong, I may continue to praise You in this life and work harder -according to my possibilities and Your will- for my own salvation and for the building of Your kingdom in this world. Amen.

105. Prayer of the sick

O Almighty and eternal God, You are my life and my health. You created every person in a perfect way and breathed into him the spirit of life (cf. Gen 2:17). Because of Adam's disobedience, however, illness was introduced and finally death.

IV Prayers in Particular Circumstances

If You want, Lord, You can heal me.

However, You, Good and Compassionate God, have not abandoned us to the power of death, but helped all men to seek and find You (cf. Eucharistic Prayer IV). In doing so, You have offered us Your help by transforming sickness and death into instruments of atonement, salvation and redemption.

If You want, Lord, You can heal me.

Turn Your radiant face upon me, a poor sinner, who cries out to You under the yoke of illness. Have compassion on me, Lord, because I am tired, because I suffer, because I feel weak and sometimes useless, because my cross weighs too much, because it hurts to be a burden to others and because at times I lack patience and the desire to live.

If You want, Lord, You can heal me.

Hence, look upon me with compassion and listen to what I ask of You. If it be Your will, if it contributes to the salvation of my soul and to Your greater glory, I beg You to grant me my total healing. Free me from the yoke of my illness. Restore me internally so I can praise You and serve You in health.

If You want, Lord, You can heal me.

Your beloved Son, Holy Father, during His mission in this world healed innumerable men and women from their diseases, and even raised many from death. Place Your hand on me and make me whole again. Lord, increase my faith in Your power. I ask this in the name of Your Son Jesus Christ in whose power I trust You will listen to my humble request.

If You want, Lord, You can heal me.

But if in Your holy will, in Your divine and unfathomable wisdom, You have already decided that my soul will benefit more from suffering this disease than enjoying health and physical well-being, I accept it and embrace it as Your Son embraced His glorious cross. I love You, my God and I praise You with deep reverence. Just give me the strength to persevere until the end. My life, God of love, is Yours. You gave it to me and You can take it from me when it pleases You. I submit myself to Your holy will with filial love, and for everything You do for me in order to bring me closer to the suffering of Your beloved Son, I praise You with deep reverence. Amen.

106. Prayer on a birthday

Almighty and ever living God, creator and redeemer of my life, You have created me for Yourself *"And my heart will remain restless until it rest in You"* (St. Augustine, Confessions).

IV Prayers in Particular Circumstances

I thank You because on a day like today (X years ago) …. You gave me the gift of seeing the light of this world for the first time. My heart praises You for all the benefits received throughout these years. Thank You for my parents, through whom You gave me life, for my family, for my friends, for so many moments of happiness, and also, Lord, thank You for the bad times, for the crosses, the humiliations, since they have made me into the man (woman) that I am today and have given me the firm certainty that You were always there when I needed You the most (cf. Hb 13: 5).

My life and my existence belong to You and I thank You for the plans You have for me. May I live this year ahead of me, if it be Your will, profoundly united to You and live it above all working out my own salvation with fear and trembling (cf. Phil 2:12). My whole life belongs to You, Lord; help me to live it by serving You and my brothers. I also ask You that after a long and full life of blessings, You may grant me the grace of a holy death in the company of Your mother Mary and my loving father Saint Joseph.

Finally, once I have crossed the threshold of this life, may I be found worthy of contemplating the beauty and majesty of Your countenance which is the supreme fulfillment of my whole existence. Amen.

107. Prayer asking for final perseverance.

My Lord and my God, great Creator of the universe, my Savior and my Redeemer, I thank You because You have created me marvelously and because You had mercy on me, forgiving me all my sins and miseries.

However, I am also aware that I must work for my own salvation with fear and trembling to persevere until the end (cf. Phil 2: 12-16). Today I am with You, but tomorrow, without Your grace, I could lose You (cf. 1 Cor 10: 12). That is why today I implore Your help so that I can walk in Your light throughout and until the end of my life.

Never deprive me of Your grace, Lord, make this grace assist me and always support me. May this grace act always in me so I can continue to faithfully respond to Your divine inspirations. May it protect me against the snares of the evil one who perseveres in his eagerness to snatch my soul into hell.

In this way, Lord, when the day of my death comes like a thief, I may not be caught unaware (cf. 2 Pt 3: 10), but on the contrary, in a diligent observance of Your commandments so I may deserve from You the crown of glory that does not wither (cf. 1Cor 9:

25). Lord, You are my salvation (cf. Ps 27: 1) without You I can do nothing (cf. Jn 15: 5). Give me, thus, Lord, I beg You, the grace of final perseverance. Amen.

108. Prayer to know how to pray correctly

Lord Jesus, You know the human heart: You formed it with Your own hands and witnessed the misery in which it fell when it moved away from You. You know, thus, how deceptive it can be. *"But You, Lord, probe the heart and examine the thoughts to give to each according to his actions and according to the fruit of his works"* (Jer 17: 9-10).

You Yourself were saddened when You encountered the Pharisees who, believing themselves to be so close to God for their intense and long prayers. However, they failed to recognize His presence in You, O Lord Jesus in Whom that same God became man for our salvation. Their long prayers were disgusting before Your eyes since their hearts were full of evil and all kinds of impurity (cf. Mt 23: 27-28).

May You never, Lord, by hearing my prayer, feel what You felt by hearing theirs. Do not let me fool myself trying to fool You. May the truth about Who You are and who I am never leave my mind. Deliver me from thinking – not even for a second - that I am good, holy or perfect. Free me from disguising my pride and my arrogance, inspired by the father of lies, with words of humility and simplicity.

You know the innermost center of my soul better than myself; You know when I sit and get up (cf. Ps 138: 1) come into the bottom of my soul, clean every corner where the devil, crouched, could hide to convince me that I am better than others and that because of that I deserve something from You.

May my prayer always be preceded by a sincere and authentic recognition of my nothingness, my filth and my unworthiness, not unlike other men, my brothers. Give me the joy to know and see myself, not as the world sees me, much less as I see myself, but as You know me and see me (cf. 1 Cor 4: 3).

Lord, I know that I do not know how to pray as I should (cf. Rom 8: 26) and that I can deceived myself in what You want from me. That is why I humbly entreat You to never let me despise the advice and the wisdom of Your Church in order to know Your true will. Give me the grace that I need so that I may always act according to Your will. May I be light for others and always practice the virtues that the Bible grants to Your closest friends and servants. Amen.

109. Prayer of humility I

Lord, God of truth, You created me from the dust of the earth and breathed into me the breath of life (cf. Gn 2: 7). My vocation is very high for my soul, but my origin is humble for my body. In not departing from this twofold truth about human nature lies true wisdom.

IV Prayers in Particular Circumstances

Hence, Lord, all the good things that I have are Your gifts and without You, I am only vanity and my weight, that of the breath of air (cf. Ps 62: 9). If all I have comes from You, then, what should I boast as I had accomplished something by myself (cf. 1 Cor 4: 7). However, because of sin, my fallen nature revolts and drives me to believe that I am not worth something separated from You. My mind is constantly attacked by lies that make me despise the truth about You and about me, falling thus into the pride that was the cause of the fall of many of Your angels.

That is why I come before You with confidence to ask for the gift of humility - without which all other virtues are useless -. Humility helps us to know who we are and Who You are, which is the base upon which our entire existence depends. Humility is also knowing that our own being is nothing more than a loan that we have received from above (cf. St. Maximus the Confessor). Give me, therefore, Lord this deep knowledge and help me to always live according to it.

Grant me to never believe myself better than others, nor that I deserve everything. And since there is no humility without humiliation, give me the patience and wisdom to endure in Your name all the humiliations which Your divine will wants or allows me to endure for my own good and for Your greatest glory.

Let me learn from You, Who being in the form of God, did not consider equality with God something to be used to Your own advantage; rather, You made Yourself nothing by taking the very nature of a servant, being made in human likeness. And being found in appearance as a man, You humbled Yourself by becoming obedient to death, even death on a cross! (cf. Phil 2: 6-11). With this same humility, I hope that - in Your mercy - You will hear my prayer not based on my merits, but on the power of Your holy Name. Amen.

110. Prayer of humility II

Who am I, Lord, without You? What do I have that You have not given me? How far I have departed from You, Lord! Accept, then, my humble praise and sincere recognition of my nothingness before Your divine majesty.

You are Creator and I am a poor creature.
You are Great and I am so insignificant.
You are Powerful and I so weak.
You are infinite Wisdom, and I am ignorant.
You are absolute freedom, and I am slave.
You are the highest Good and I am so full of misery.
You are inaccessible Light, and I am so filled with darkness.
You are the Source of life and I am so empty of everything.
You are Eternal and I so ephemeral.
You are Holy and I am such a sinner.
You are Rich and I am so poor.
You are Perfection itself and I am so full of defects.
You are a loving Father, and I am a rebellious son.
You are sovereign King, and I am a useless servant.
You are Most High above all and I am capable of such lowness.

IV Prayers in Particular Circumstances

You are Immovable like a rock, and I am so fickle and changing.
You are the Truth, and I am such a friend of lies.

Let us pray

Lord, Almighty God, in Your image and likeness, You created me with great wonder and beauty (cf. Gen 1: 26). By my own freedom, however, I moved away from You and became despicable. Have mercy on me, a sinner, and help me to always come back to You. Assist me, through Your grace, to recover in me, all the gifts with which You created men and never let me forget that apart from You, I can do nothing (cf. Jn 15: 4-5). Thus, make me perfect, like You, Great God, are perfect (cf. Mt 5:48). Amen.

111. Prayer of Thanksgiving for a favor granted

Lord Jesus, I thank You for listening to me. You have accepted with pleasure my poor prayer and You have not been deaf to my supplication, for that I sincerely thank You (cf. Ps 6: 9).

The moment of the test for now has been mitigated, and in the middle of my darkness You have sent me a ray of light. You are a Good and Just God and no one who hopes in You will ever be put to shame, once again I thank You (cf. Ps 25: 3).

Forgive me because maybe at the time of the test I was afraid, because I did not fully trust You, because I got discouraged, because I doubted Your power, in a word for having had so little faith (cf. Mk 4: 40. 6, 6; Mt 8: 26; Lk 8: 25). Therefore, I acknowledge, Lord, that Your commandments are just that You rightly made me suffer (cf. Sal 119: 75). And for not getting tired of me, for Your unconditional love and for Your unwavering fidelity and patience, I give You thanks.

Now I ask You not to let me forget You, to always remember that all I have is Your gift and that, therefore, You can take it away from me at any time. For being aware that I depend on You, for knowing that all I have is Yours, my heart infinitely thank You.

Help me to always value Your divine gifts, to be grateful for them and, since all I have belongs to You, dispose of it when and how You wish. O God of infinite goodness! One thing I ask of You, if in Your infinite wisdom You decide to test me once again, as You just did, help me to increase my faith and my confidence in Your power. In those moments, even if You decided to take everything away from me, I beg You never, God of my life, to take away the joy of Your paternal company. Amen.

112. Prayer of a prisoner

Jesus, patient and suffering Lord, from the depths of my life, I cry out to You with the confidence that in You I will find mercy and compassion. Listen, then, to my prayer. My

IV Prayers in Particular Circumstances

limitations, my mistakes and my sins have brought me to my present situation in which I find myself deprived of my freedom. I know, Good Lord, that You, better than anyone, understand me, since You were also imprisoned. The difference is that You were deprived of Your freedom due to the greatest injustice ever committed. I, on the other hand; suffer precisely what I deserve for my crimes (cf. Lk 23: 41).

Accept, Lord, my sincere and humble confession and listen to me, not because I am good, but because You are. That's why I come to You, to beg You to help me. First, I want to ask You to transform me from within, change my heart, heal my wounds, touch my past and restore me. Lord, You created me good not bad. Grant me, I beg You, that during this time and in this place, I may seek You and find You. My true chains are not those that I carry in this prison, but those with which I have enslaved my soul, my spirit and my mind. By Your power, set me free me from them. Without You the freedom that I misused only served me to make me a slave to myself and to others.

Lord, my sins led me to cause much harm to many people. I ask You especially for those, whom I hurt with my crimes, help them, repair the damage I did to them, give them much more than what I took from them with my selfishness, and heal their hearts from all hatred towards me. Have them forgive me to find peace. I also ask You for my family; I beg You to help them, console them, assist them, do not let them forget me, provide for them what is necessary for living and never allow that anything bad happens to them.

And to me, Lord, give me the patience and serenity to do my time in peace. Help me not to get into trouble. Do not allow my situation to be further complicated, deliver me from all evil. Protect me from those who want to harm me. Make me a sign of Your love in the midst of those who, like me, live here deprived of their freedom.

I express to You, solemnly, that it is my will to change my life and become my best self; You have convinced me that it is never too late. This time, however, I do not want my life and my freedom so that I can do what I want, but in order to live it out, from now on, praising and loving You for all the times in the past I refused to do so. I want to serve You, Lord, and I will do it diligently. O sweet Lord You are Good; Your love endures forever and Your faithfulness continues through all generations (cf. Ps 100: 5). Amen.

113. Prayer of those suffering from same sex attraction

Lord God of infinite wisdom, mercy, love and tenderness, You have created the universe and filled it with greatness and majesty. Everything that Your hand has done is full of perfection and beauty, so that You never regret anything You have created. Your hand formed human beings from the dust of the earth, man and woman You formed them (cf. Gen 1:27). Unlike the beasts of the field, You endowed them with intelligence, will and freedom, so that they would not be dominated by the power of their passions. In this way, after Your work of

IV Prayers in Particular Circumstances

creation was finished, You were pleased to contemplate it because You saw that it was very good (cf. Gen 1:31).

Sin, however, introduced disorder and confusion into the work of Your hands and among its many consequences caused man and woman to move away from You, exchanging the natural use of sexuality for one against nature, thus receiving in his own flesh the very consequences of his loss (cf. Rom 1: 26-27). Lord of infinite goodness, turn, then, Your merciful and compassionate countenance toward all those of us suffering from same sex attraction.

Only You, Lord, know our sufferings and our loneliness. Only You can see the causes and deep wounds that lie at the root of these inclinations. Only You know our hearts even better than us. Have mercy on us, Lord!

We thank You for the many talents and gifts we have received from Your generous hand. We also thank You for Your Word and for Your holy Church. By them, we know that it is not Your will that we live according to these inclinations and needs that oppose the natural order that, in Your wisdom and perfection, You have established in human sexuality.

We ask You, then, with deep humility, to give us the strength so that, driven by Your grace, we can live in perfect chastity making of You our only love. By Your power show us that which is impossible for men, is within reach of those who, like us, put all our trust in You. Help us to find in Your Church, a mother, always ready to welcome us with open arms to understand our struggles and raise us up when we fall.

Help and convert the hearts of all those, our brothers and sisters who, deceived by the world, the devil and their own flesh, live according to these inclinations and, therefore, closed to Your Divine Grace. Have mercy on them too, Lord! We love them and want them to be saved.

And to us, assist us to be living witnesses that You are enough to fill the human heart. Let everyone know that You do not define men or women by their weaknesses, but by their dignity and by the love You have for them. May the whole world know that only in You and in faithful obedience to Your mandates lies the true peace and the true balance that makes every human being find his true happiness. Lord, You know everything, You know that we love You (cf. Jn 21:17). Amen.

114. Prayer of forgiveness of those who have offended us

Lord God, eternal King and Merciful Father Whom I have offended countless times and from Whom I have always received mercy and forgiveness, today I come before You to ask You to teach me how to forgive.

You have taught us to forgive those who have offended us (cf. Mt 6: 12) up to seventy times seven (cf. Mt 18: 22), to turn the other cheek, to give to those who ask us and to pray for those who slander

IV Prayers in Particular Circumstances

us (cf. Lk 6: 28-30). Lord may Your name be always blessed!

The pain of the betrayal and the offenses committed by those in whom I had placed my trust, has hurt my heart and left in it wounds that have filled me with bitterness to the point of making me think of revenge.

But my heart belongs to You and being Yours there can be neither hate nor resentment in it. Aware, then, of my weakness I come to Your presence to implore You to heal me.

Help me to do good in return for all the evil done to me. Help my heart so that, resembling Yours, I may will not only the temporary good of those who have done me wrong, but above all their eternal salvation. Teach me to forgive as You forgave from the cross those who crucified You (cf. Lk 23: 34).

I know that You, Patient and Good as You are, will give time to heal my wounds; I thank You for this. But today, I want to show You my firm intention to forgive even in spite of these wounds. You were innocent and without blemish, and yet forgave Your enemies, help this sinner and wretch whom You have forgiven so much, forgive those who, like me, suffer under the law of sin in this world. Amen.

115. Prayer at the beginning of fasting

Lord Jesus, God of love and mercy, in this propitious time of penance and prayer I want to offer You today this fasting. You Yourself, Lord, in preparation for Your mission, spent forty days and nights in the desert without food (cf. Lk 4: 2). In this way, You overpowered the insidious attacks of the enemy, the devil. Strengthen my body to be able to resist the privation of nourishment in order to be renewed in the spirit (cf. Jl 2:12). May this act of penance help me overcome the terrible demons that insist in their efforts to make me fall. You, merciful Lord, have taught me that these kinds of demons can only be expelled through prayer and fasting (cf. Mt 9:21).

Help me, during this time of fasting, to show myself filled with the joy of being Your disciple and not appear before people sad or with my face disfigured with the purpose of being noticed by men and thus receive from them their praise (cf. Mt 6: 17). You and only You, Lord, are my reward. And if athletes deprive themselves of pleasures to get a withering crown, with more reason I am willing to deprive myself of nourishment in order to gain a crown that does not wither (cf. 1 Cor 9: 25). May this sacrifice help me to understand that this world with its riches passes and that only You are necessary. Lord, You sacrificed Your life for my salvation; accept this small and insignificant sacrifice as propitiation for my sins and for my own sanctification. Amen.

IV Prayers in Particular Circumstances

116. Prayer of a penitent going to confession after many years

Lord and Good Father, here You have me humbly recognizing that I have sinned against heaven and against You, to tell You that I do not deserve to call myself Your son (cf. Lk 15:21).

Many years ago, I left Your house and walked away from Your love. I was rebellious, disobedient; I lost interest in You and let myself be devoured by the empty glories of this world.

For a time, I live in sin I did what I wanted, when and how I wanted it. There was nothing of which I deprived myself. But after trying all these pleasures, little by little everything tasted so bitter, everything was so empty. I was looking for happiness and only found sadness. I became miserable and brought misery to those around me.

But now I come before You to implore Your forgiveness and Your mercy. Your ministers have told me that You are Good and, in this certainty, I have placed all my hope.

All this time spent without You, my soul has become ill, my eyes blind to my sins, my ears deaf to Your calls and my heart indifferent to Your sufferings. Thinking that I was dining on succulent delicacies, I realized I was feeding on the pods of the pigs (cf. Lk 15: 16). Have mercy on me, O Lord!

Prayers of the Soul

This sacramental confession that You have inspired me to make today, I have made with deep faith, but I know it is only the beginning. Therefore, I pledge to continue examining my conscience and to return each month to confession, in order to cleanse my soul and purify my spirit from all these years in which I moved away from Your love.

I pledge to look for You in daily prayer, to know You better through the study of my faith and to live according to Your commands for Your greater glory and for my own salvation. Help me to better appreciate and benefit from all the goods that You have deposited in Your holy Catholic Church and from which I deprived myself all these years. I humbly implore You to stay with me, Lord.

Grant me please the strength and the courage to start over; I want to be only Yours. And now that I have returned to Your house, Good Father, do not ever let me leave again because what would be the use of gaining the whole world, if I lose my soul by living far away from You (cf. Mt 16:26). Amen.

117. Prayer of liberation from the sin of pride and arrogance

Lord Jesus, God of truth, You know the intentions of men and scrutinize every heart; have compassion on this servant of Yours burdened under the weight of pride and arrogance. Come and save me!

IV Prayers in Particular Circumstances

It was at the very beginning of time, even before the origin of humanity, that one of Your angels, dragging others in his delirium, had the insolence of rebelling against You by opposing Your divine will. This was the first sin, sin of arrogance and pride, spiritual sin, the most terrible, fatal cause that a huge crowd of Your most perfect spiritual beings were thrown into the abyss of the earth where even You, Infinite Goodness, were forced to create unfathomable hells where these fallen angels, now turned into horrendous demons, would dwell forever without any hope of redemption (cf. Mt 25: 41; 2 Pt 2: 4; Is 14: 12).

Look at me with compassion, Lord, I beseech You. I am full of pride and arrogance to such an extent that I find it so hard to recognize. Many times, I have fought my ego, but I have been defeated. This has led me, not only to close the doors of Your forgiveness, but also to hurt people I love, dragging them into the most frightening misery. My blindness is profound, Lord; these spiritual sins make me believe myself superior to others, while hiding behind a false humility and an apparent spiritual life. I resemble those Pharisees against whom You uttered terrible words of condemnation (cf. Mt 23: 13, 12).

I know very well that none of the virtues that I can practice will help my salvation, as long as these sins of the spirit rule in my soul. While the sinner, whatever his sin is, if he repents and comes to You, he will be saved; the arrogant, on the other hand, dominated by the art of lies, not only deceives himself, but also pretends to deceive You.

Save me, Lord, from this great sin; come, enter my soul with all Your strength, remove my stony heart and forge in its place a new heart, a heart of flesh, capable of true piety (cf. Ez 36: 26). Show me the true path, put light in my darkness. Deliver me from a life of lies. By Your grace prevent me from falling into the abyss of my ego and remove from my soul all falsehood and hypocrisy.

Your precious gift of time is what it has prevented Your justice from sending me to meet with Satan and his angels. Your mercy has postponed the day of my death, so I still have time. For this, Lord, I infinitely thank You.

Therefore, God of tenderness and mercy, I bow down before You, with all that I am and I have to implore You, from where my soul joins with my spirit, that I am willing to endure all kinds of humiliations, sufferings, diseases and crosses, whatever is necessary, in order to eradicate from my soul this sin of Lucifer.

Accept me, Lord, as the last of Your servants. Grant that I always seek spiritual guides, who, instead of praising my false devotion, may correct me and encourage me in the constant struggle against myself -my worst enemy-. By Your precious Blood, by Your most holy cross, by Your loving Mother, by Your love for humanity, do not forsake me. And above all, do not put an end to my life while I am still slave of the worst of all vices: the pride of the spirit. Amen.

IV Prayers in Particular Circumstances

118. Prayer of renunciation

Almighty and ever-living God, Victorious King, prostrated before Your Divine Majesty I promise to renounce to *(mention what it is being renounced)* ... I trust that the sacrifice of this - which is so dear to me - will be pleasing to You as was the sacrifice of Abraham, Your servant (cf. Gen 22: 2).

The reasons why You ask me to offer You this great sacrifice are now hidden to my limited intelligence. You know that separating me from this causes my soul the deepest pain and the most unspeakable suffering, but I trust in Your divine will that this shall be the best for me and the most helpful to Your plan of salvation.

Give me the strength to be able, not only to give up what You ask of me, but to offer it willingly, thus practicing the perfect obedience that You like so much. You are God and that is why You are entitled to everything that I have and possess, including myself. You know You can take away anything I have and that You want from me at any time. Just give me the grace to always be faithful and never suffer the misfortune to separate myself from You. Amen.

119. Prayer in time of loneliness

O God of love and compassion, Father all-powerful, Christ Lord and Savior, Spirit of love and consolation, I praise You for Your wisdom, Your will and Your justice:. You are One and Triune God, perfect unity in diversity of persons, divine and transcendent Majesty. I thank You for creating me after Your image and likeness.

O Lord, I feel lonely, forgotten and despised. I do not blame anyone for this, but myself and that is why I ask You to forgive me. Loneliness is very sad, Lord, but also very dangerous, since not only does it sadden the spirit, but it can be an opportunity for the enemy to act in the soul.

Therefore, I come to You, God of all consolation. Look at me with compassion, do not forsake me, enter within me, dwell in my soul and fill my spirit. Make me feel Your love by making me remember so many favors received from Your hand throughout my life.

When time came where Jesus was about to give everything up to the point of giving Himself for love of humankind, Your beloved Son also experienced loneliness, when He was rejected by the world, and even by His own friends.

IV Prayers in Particular Circumstances

May I experience the same sentiments of Your beloved Son in every moment of loneliness and abandonment. Do not let me despair, or be sad, and above all, do not let me feel a victim of anything, or anyone.

Help me to accept what I cannot change, to change what Your grace enables me to change and to feel the peace of knowing that I am totally in Your hands.

In spite of my loneliness, give me the grace to be joyful, to always be willing to offer a smile, to extend a helping hand to those who are in most need - those who experience a loneliness which is even deeper than mine -. In a word, assist me to think of others and their pains rather than mine. I place these intentions into Your loving and caring hands; I know that You are always with me (cf. Jn 8:29). *"I love You, Lord, You are my strength"* (Ps 18: 1). Amen.

120. Prayer during moments of anguish and anxiety

God of hope and consolation, Prince of peace, You suffered anguish, uncertainty and anxiety more than any other human being. That night in the garden, before being delivered to Your passion, on the cold rock - which symbolized our stony hearts - You sweat Blood and begged Your Father to deliver You from drinking such a bitter cup (cf. Mt 26: 39). Kindly turn the beauty of Your countenance towards this poor sinner who agonizes in anguish.

"My soul is full of misfortune and my life is on the edge of the abyss" (Ps 87: 1). An intense anxiety haunts me and I am afraid of what might happen to me. Unlike You, innocent and immaculate Lamb, I do deserve these anguishes, if not because I have caused them, certainly for my many sins and my many rebellions, ignored by all, but known only to You.

Come to my soul, oh beloved Shepherd. Open the waters of the sea of my vicissitudes so that I may pass victorious as the people of Israel once did through the Red Sea. Calm down my spirit, as You calmed the stormy waters of the Sea of Galilee. Give me the peace and joy with which You appeased the troubled hearts of Your disciples on the glorious morning of Your resurrection.

You, Who freed so many from the devil, cast out from me the snares of the evil one. Give me the confidence You gave to all those You cured, and even returned to life.

I want to see, Lord, what You see. I want to hear, Lord, what You hear. I want to think, Lord, as You think. Give me the peace that comes from knowing that all the hairs of my head are numbered and that not one will fall if You do not allow it (cf. Mt

IV Prayers in Particular Circumstances

10:30). I beg You, O Lord, to grant me the certainty that my name is written on the palm of Your hand (cf. Is 49: 16) and that even if my own mother abandoned me, Lord, You will never forsake me (cf. Is 49, 15).

Good God, my physical and spiritual enemies seek my ruin, fight with me. Do not abandon me in the midst of this tribulation, because if You are with me, who can stand against me (cf. Rom 8: 31). Finally, God of infinite tenderness, in these moments of anguish I humbly entreat You to give me the assurance that whoever hopes in You will never be disappointed (cf. Ps 25: 3). Jesus, I trust in You. Amen.

121. Prayer for addiction deliverance

Almighty and ever-living God for You nothing is impossible (cf. Lk 1:37). I bow down before You with deep humility, knowing my many limitations and miseries, to implore from You the healing of my mind and my body. Deliver me, then, Lord, from this addiction that enslaves me, that corrodes my life and prevents me from being happy.

From You, Good and Merciful God, comes true and authentic freedom, the same freedom You gave me but that I lost because I abandoned You. Indeed, I despised You, source of living water and set off in search of cracked cisterns (cf. Jr 2: 13). I have lived according to my bad decisions and loved a deceptive and perverse world. In this way, I departed from You and seeking to be freed, I fell slave to false gods. This is how I find myself in a prison which I have tried to escape many times, only to fall right back into it again.

I recognize that alone I cannot get out of this addiction and that silence and secrecy are my worst enemies. But I am afraid of public shame and of losing everything I have. That is why I come before You and abandon myself totally to Your will; I will do what You tell me to regain my freedom, which I can only find by Your side.

Listen to me, Lord, and free me from this terrible dependence on *(name the addiction)* ... With Your Divine Grace balance my mind, heal my body with the power of Your hand, and cover me with Your shadow AND HEAL ME BY YOUR MERCY. May my will become strong and so free myself from these chains of death. May my will, once restored by Your Grace, only have the goal of pleasing You in this life and obtaining by Your same Grace the life that You have promised me. In Your name I trust, my Lord and my God, my Rock, my Defender and my Deliverer! (cf. Ps 18: 2). Amen.

122. Prayer to begin again after falling out from grace

Lord Jesus, my Compassionate and Pious Redeemer, *"... against You, You only, have I sinned, and done this evil in thy sight"* (Ps 50: 6).

IV Prayers in Particular Circumstances

How much weariness and discouragement lies now in my soul, Lord; I fell again into the same sin. Great discouragement and great sadness nest in my heart when I see that my purposes of living in Your grace do not give results. How weak and how fragile I am, Lord!

I would like to give up and not fight anymore, call the good bad and the bad good, and stay here in the mud, in the filth. The devil presents me with a thousand reasons not to continue, to abandon Your narrow path and walk the wide path where he has led so many souls (cf. Mt 7: 13). He says to me: "You can no longer keep trying, you are not happy, God will understand, follow this wide path, if you listen to me you will no longer feel this sadness that now disturbs your soul." And I say to him: *"Get behind me Satan!"* (Mt 16: 23).

How can I follow his path if I know that it will only lead me to perdition? How can I leave You? Where will I go, Lord, if only You have words of eternal life? (cf. Jn 6:68). And I say to myself, how can I stay on the ground, if I have seen You getting up three times from Your falls, under the heavy wood of the cross? Your falls are not due to Your faults, because You have none, O Immaculate Lamb! They are due to mine and yet You get up, take Your cross and move on. How can I, then, stay on the floor? Therefore, Lord, I will begin again.

You do not get tired of forgiving me and You always offer me Your kind hand. How can I be discouraged if You always wait for me from the cross with open arms to embrace me, heal me, dress me and restore my lost dignity? (cf. Lk 15:22) Therefore, Lord, I will begin again!

How could I stay in the mud of my miseries, when I see You whipped and crowned with thorns for the sole purpose that I may rise, follow You and one day be crowned with glory in heaven? Therefore, Lord, I will begin again!

After confessing my sins and receiving Your forgiveness by the consecrated hands of Your priest, I will begin once more, Lord! I do it because, even when You were crucified and suffering unspeakable pain, You did not lose heart to the point of abandoning Your cross knowing that I was going to fail You. No! You stayed there for love of me, waiting for me. How can I get discouraged then? Hence, Lord, I will begin again!

I will do it because You have stayed in the Eucharist so that I may find You always near me and obtain the strength to rise. Therefore, Lord, I will begin again!

I will do it because I know that I am not alone. You are with me and with Your power You will help me pick up my life from the ground, shattered by my selfishness, and rebuild it piece by piece again making it anew as when it came out of Your hand. Therefore, Lord, I will begin again!

Because You love me, because You are Good, because time exists as a gift of Your love so I can always in this life start over, because Your grace is powerful and has no limits and because *"... Your mercy is eternal and higher than the heavens"* (Ps 103:11). Therefore, Lord, I will begin again!

I will begin again to adore You, to serve You, to receive You in Holy Communion, and to have You as a guest in my soul. There I will become Your Temple and within me I will embrace You with the certain hope that Your love will never fail me even I do fail You again. For all this, Lord, I will begin again! Amen.

123. Prayer in moments of temptation of the flesh

Lord Jesus, by the grace of the most pure womb that carried You, by the merits of all the saints, merits that come from You, O uncreated Grace, have mercy on me and listen to my humble prayer. I humbly invoke Your help in this unfortunate hour, so as not to succumb to the temptations of the evil one. This ancient serpent, father of all lies prowls around like a roaring lion looking to devour me (cf. 1 Pet 5:8). Give me the right words that, like You in the desert, I may reject this infernal beast, enemy of the human race and Your redemptive work (cf. Mt 4:1-11). Send to my heart Your Spirit of fortitude, wisdom, counsel, as well as Your Spirit of fear of God so as not to fall into the traps of the one who seeks so forcefully my downfall.

Good Shepherd, You know the weakness of my flesh, have mercy on me. Embrace me with Your love, protect me with Your name, be my bastion, my refuge, my saving rock, my strength and my light (cf. 2 Sam 22:2). Send in front of me in this very moment

Saint Michael the Archangel, prince of the heavenly armies. Do not leave me fighting this battle alone, because I will surely succumb.

Help me to see with Your eyes the superfluous, the banal, the vile, the empty and the ephemeral of this maleficent fruit, which is now presented to me as an exquisite good, but which is nothing more than a pestilent poison that will destroy me. Lord Jesus, have mercy on me, give me the grace I need to strengthen my miserable and weak will, that it may embrace You and take refuge in You like a chick under the wings of her mother (cf. Mt 23: 37).
(Moment of silence for God to act)

Once the temptation has been rejected, give me, Lord of consolations, faith and firmness to mortify my flesh, which will torture me with reproaches for not having given it what it was asking with such eagerness. Give me the strength to resist and to live by faith and hope, not in this world that passes, but in Your Word that does not fail. I believe in You, Lord, and I know that whoever waits on You will not be disappointed, *qui sustinent te, non confundentur* (cf. Ps 25: 3).

Finally, help me to be attentive, because the accuser and his angels will regroup their armies and return again with greater fury and will not give up, because as long as I live, their only mission is to snatch my soul to the pit where there is no hope.

Make me hate sin, my Lord, and never forget that its salary is and always will be death *"stipendia enim peccati mors"* (Rom 6: 23). Amen.

124. Prayer asking protection against the Devil

Lord Jesus, You are the holy one, I humbly beg You to protect me, my loved ones and my entire home from the power and insidious attacks of the evil one, that rebellious angel, that ancient serpent who is the enemy of the human race and whose mission is to spoil Your saving work and who is always searching for whom to devour (cf. 1 Pet 5: 8).

Do not let him, Lord, besiege my home. Come with Your power and Your Holy Spirit and throw him back once again into hell. Send us the Archangel Saint Michael, prince of Your heavenly armies, in order to make Satan and all his angels flee from here.

Without Your help I will perish in this fight, but with Your assistance I know that I will have nothing to fear. Take away his dark and maleficent presence from every corner of this house, from every member of my family, from every object and pet that belongs to this household.

Place Your sacred seal on the door of my house so that the power of hell knows that each and every one of those who live here have been bought with Your Precious Blood and thus they belong only to You. God of power and glory under Your Holy Name I solemnly place the spiritual wellbeing of my soul and that of my entire family. Amen.

125. Prayer in preparation for an imminent death

Almighty and ever living God, Merciful and Compassionate Father, Yours are life and death, from You we come and to You, at the end of our lives, we return; Your power is sovereign over of all that exists.

I come to You at the end of my life to thank You. First of all, I want to thank You for the opportunity to be aware of this imminent moment of my death. With this magnanimous gesture, You show, in a special way, Your solicitude and Your love for me, a poor sinner.

For this great mercy of Your love, I am able to - with Your grace - be better prepared to begin my transit back home, O Good Father! Accept with gratitude my deep, reverent and filial submission to Your holy will and with it, my firm confession that You are the Lord of heaven and earth and all that is contained in them (cf. Ps 24: 1).

Good Lord, it has always been my conviction that You have given me this life to revere You, serve You and give You glory and thus save my soul (cf. St. Ignatius of Loyola, Spiritual Exercises). In these

IV Prayers in Particular Circumstances

moments I experience - as is natural - a fear of death, but at the same time I know that *"... although I walk through dark valleys, I fear no danger, because You are at my side; Your rod and Your staff support me"* (Ps 23: 4). I also know that both weather in life or in death, I belong to You, Lord (cf. Rom 14: 8).

I trust You and I am convinced that neither death nor life, neither angels nor demons, neither the present nor the future, nor any powers, neither height nor depth, nor anything else in all creation, will be able to separate me from Your love that is in Christ Jesus my Lord (cf. Rom 8: 38-39). That is why I confess with total hope that death is not the end, but the beginning of the future life and that since I lived in You all my life, death for me will be a total gain (cf. Phil 1:21).

I also confess with fear and trembling that upon leaving this world, the terrible Judgment of Your Majesty awaits me (cf. Heb 9: 27), a Judgment of absolute justice, a Judgment of full truth, but also a Judgment of unwavering love.

For this reason, I beg You, now that I have not yet crossed the threshold of this world, to have mercy on me, to help me prepare myself through all the sacramental and spiritual aid You have entrusted to Your holy Church. I beg You to please give me this grace to be able to leave this world being Your son (daughter), holy and irreproachable, with nothing in my soul that could displease You.

But if this was not possible - since nothing impure can come into Your presence (cf. Rev 21:27) - and I leave this world, free from sin, but with wounds and imperfections in my heart, help me, O Lord of goodness, to make my passage through purgatory brief. There, in the company of the blessed souls, may I receive the graces that, at that moment, I will no longer be able to attain by myself. In this way, after being purified by the fire of Your love and Your justice, may I soon, Good Lord, contemplate the beauty of Your face in Your eternal kingdom.

But before leaving this world, help me, loving Shepherd, to reconcile myself with my family and my friends, to beg forgiveness from those I have offended and to forgive in my heart those who have hurt me. Do not let my heart be closed in resentment and hatred. Deliver me from pride, a sin that closes the doors of Your mercy.

I ask You, Lord, also, to grant me the grace of final perseverance in keeping intact the Catholic, Apostolic and Roman faith that I embraced in my baptism. Protect me from the snares of the devil and his demons that will do everything possible, in these last moments, to snatch my soul to hell. Send Your angels to protect me from any temptation of either presumption or despair. May Mary Most Holy, and my father, Saint Joseph, as well as my guardian angel and all the holy angels accompany me in my transit and may I close my eyes to this world with the same peace with which Your saints and Your martyrs closed theirs. Holy Father, in Your hands I entrust my spirit! (cf. Lk 23: 46) and from my dead bed I beg You to *"... remember me when You come into Your kingdom"* (Lk 23:42). Amen.

V EXTRA PRAYERS

Our Lady of Perpetual Help

V Extra Prayers

126. Prayer while taking off in an airplane

"Our Father who art in heaven hallowed be thy name" (Mt 6: 9), these same heavens declare the glory of Your Name, and the sky above proclaims Your handiwork (cf. Ps 19: 1) You sit above the circle of the earth, and its inhabitants are like grasshoppers; You stretch out the heavens like a curtain, and spread them like a tent to dwell in (cf. Is 40:22). *"When I behold Your heavens, the work of Your fingers, the moon and the stars, which You set in place— what is man that You are mindful of him, or the son of man that You care for him?..."* (Ps 8: 3-4). Indeed, Lord, *"... who can number the clouds by wisdom? Or who can tilt the water skins of the heavens"* (Jb 38:37).

For all of these, Lord, I give You thanks. Moreover, I praise Your name because for Your great glory, You have given mankind, created in Your image, the intelligence and the ability to invent and build machines capable of cruising the heavens, shortening the distances and bringing people together. From up here we realize, in a very special way, how awesome Your creation is as well as how great You have fashioned the human mind. Furthermore, from up here we realize how fragile, small and helpless we are in comparison to the power and greatness of Your creation.

That is why, Lord, as I praise You by gazing at Your wonders, I also humbly ask You to protect me and those who travel with me on this journey. Give us good weather so that our trip may be smooth and peaceful. Give the pilots the tranquility and concentration they need to take us safely to our destination. Do not allow any human error to endanger our lives. May Your hand lead us in safety to have a successful landing. Bless and assist in their work all the crew members of this aircraft.

I also ask Your grace and protection for all the passengers aboard. Even though we travel together, we walk on so many different paths. Maybe some of them believe in You but not fully, others, for many circumstances, may have decided to keep You out of their lives and still others may not even know You. Come into their minds and change their hearts so they may have eternal life which can only come by knowing You, the one true God, and Jesus Christ, Whom You have sent (cf. Jn 7:3). Do not allow any of us on this airplane to be now as close to heaven as we are ever going to get. Deliver all of us here and now from the presence of the evil one that his attacks and temptations may not reach any of us.

Lord of heavens, come with us on this trip and give all of us the grace of one day being found worthy of contemplating Your Son *"... coming with the clouds of the skies with great power and glory to gather His elect from the four winds, from the ends of the earth to the ends of heaven...."* (Rev 1:7; Mk 3:26-27) Amen.

V Extra Prayers

127. Prayer before an important meeting

Father of unity and harmony with profound love and humility we invoke Your assistance at the beginning of this meeting that is about to take place.

Send over us Your Holy Spirit so that we can find common ground and avoid all division. Help us to see the value of diversity and the richness of thinking different from each other. We know that *"… as the body is one though it has many parts, and all the parts of the body, though many are one body, so also Christ (…) But God has so constructed the body as to give greater honor to a part that is without it, so that there may be no division in the body, but that the parts may have the same concern for one another"* (1 Cor 12: 12. 22-26). Hence, Lord of goodness and kindness, grant us the grace of learning from each other, knowing that we all have something to contribute.

Despite the fact that we are different from each other we all share in the same faith which You have given us in the person of Your Son Jesus and passed on to us through Your Holy Church. O Beloved Lord of everything that exists let peace reign in our meeting. Give us the courage to speak the truth but always in charity ever mindful that You live not only among us but in each one of us. Help us that in our participation we may speak and act as Your disciples, it is to say as messengers of peace and reconciliation. Enlighten our hearts and our minds to always see the positive before the negative.

Help us during the progress of this meeting to seek Your will as our priority and put ours in the second place. Assist us to be humble and free us from being arrogant and thinking that we know everything. Once we have discovered Your will help us to put it into practice with promptitude and joy. Give us the grace to work not only for earthly goals but to achieve our salvation and the salvation of all men and women. We ask this through Our Lord Jesus Christ Your Son. Amen.

128. Prayer of a police officer

Almighty and ever living God, Lord of peace and power, I place myself under Your protection. You have called me to safeguard the safety of the public and for that I give You thanks. Help me to do my job with professionalism and efficiency. I am aware that because of the nature of my job, my life and my safety are often in peril but I know that You are always with me and in Your protection I have put my trust. Keep Satan and his demons away from the minds and the lives of the people I serve in this community.

Give me the grace that I may always respect everyone regardless of their race, religion, social status or culture. Do not ever allow racism, discrimination or hatred to influence the service my partners and I perform in the community. Help us to show those who do not trust us that we are here to serve and protect.

Lord, You are faithful; You are my protector and I know You will defend me from the evil one (cf. 2 Thes 3:3). Grant me also the necessary graces to be always ready when You decide to call me to Your kingdom. Good Lord, I humbly ask You to protect my family and all of those who, like me, have dedicated their lives to law enforcement, serving the public and common good. Amen.

129. Prayer of healing for those who have been sexually abused

O God of mercy and compassion I come before You trusting in Your love and solicitude. You know my heart, You know my suffering, and You know my pain. You are the Lord of my past, my present and my future and everything I am and I have is Yours.

I come before You with profound humility carrying on my shoulders the heavy weight of the abuse I was inflicted, in order to implore from You assistance and healing. Many years ago I was a victim of sexual abuse, somebody preyed on me and taking advantage of me stole my innocence and negatively affected my life forever. Since then, I have lived my life as best as I could but immersed in so much pain and suffering. I am broken from within and I have had to fight against these memories by myself in silence. This has made my life extremely difficult and many times unbearable.

Often, I asked myself: where were You God? Why did You allow this to happen to me? Why did You not defend me from this evil when I could not do it by myself? And I do not find a clear answer. However, I know You are Good and that You did not want this to happen to me, yet You allowed it, so that from the worst situation You can bring about so much good. Then, I look at Your Son, the innocent Lamb, who was slaughtered by our sins and how much suffering this sacrifice, caused You, yet You allowed it because You knew that through this terrible crime, Your Son, by obedience and sacrifice, would bring about the salvation of all humanity.

Because I want to unite myself to the cross of Jesus, I come to You, O Father, to ask You, to beg You, to implore You, have mercy on me, Lord, and send Your Holy Spirit to cure me from this trauma, free me from these chains of terror and pain, and heal my wounds so I can be whole again.

I ask You especially to help me, O Lord, to do what has been until now so hard for me to do, which is to forgive the one who did this to me. *(if the person*

V Extra Prayers

is still alive the following is said... Do not allow him (her) to do it to anybody else and give me discernment and courage so I may know how I can help to stop him (her) from doing it to somebody else).

I ask You to please protect every child, every young man and woman from predators. Do not let any innocent person endure what I had to suffer. *(If You have children the following is said* Help me to take good care of my children and always be vigilant and attentive to any danger to which they could be exposed).

Nothing is impossible for You, O Lord. Help me with Your grace to become like You and to live my life so I can be a perfect example of Your love, mercy and forgiveness in the world. That I may be like Jesus willing to embrace my cross for the salvation of others. I humbly ask You to help me keep the true faith and persevere in it until the end. I ask You most specially to free the Church from predators and to bring to justice to those leaders who covered up their crimes.

I love You, Lord, without You I can do nothing. All of these I ask in the name of Your Son, Jesus Christ Who is my Lord, my Savior and my Healer, my Fortress, and the Rock in Whom I take refuge (cf. Ps 94:22). Amen.

130. Prayer of protection before a natural disaster

Lord and Master of all Creation in Your power and might, You laid the foundation of the earth (cf. Jb 38:4) we humbly ask Your protection in this time of tribulation.

Nature threatens with its fury our homes, our possessions and even our own lives. With Your sovereign power intervene so that the wrath of nature recedes, thus submitting itself to Your holy and powerful will.

At the beginning of the Old Covenant, You saved Your people from the power of Pharaoh and with the breath of Your mouth made the waters go back making the Sea into dry land, dividing the waters of the ocean and so making Your people cross between walls of waters (Ex 14: 21-22).

Moreover, in the New Covenant You calmed down the waters and winds that threatened Your disciples in the Sea of Galilee and even walked on its turbulent waters. Therefore, Lord of Power and Might, come to our aid and deliver us from this coming disaster (cf. Mk 4:45-51; Jn 6:16-24). Protect our homes, our families, our children, our animals, our crops, everything that is important to us and that has cost us so much labor and expense.

But above all, do not let the violence of nature claim any human life among us. Help us understand that the ultimate reason for which nature groans with labor pains lies in its effort to be freed from sin which subjected it (cf. Rom 8:32).

Therefore, help us that by believing in You and living a holy life guided by Your grace, we may be pleasing to Your eyes and never deserve the punishment of disobedient children (cf. Jon 1:1). That having been freed from this tribulation we can say with the psalmist: *"He has not treated us according to our sins, nor paid us according to our iniquities"* (Ps 103: 10). Lord, we praise You and bless You, the heavens declare Your glory and the heights proclaim the work of Your hands (Ps 9: 1). Amen.

131. Prayer of a soldier

Lord Jesus, faithful guardian of our salvation, I want to thank You for having called me to serve my country by defending it from alien foes. You God are a God of peace not a God of war, (cf. Jgs 6:24; 1 Cor 14:33; Rom 15:33. 16:20; 2 Cor 13:11; Phi 4:9; Heb 13:20. I ask You first of all for peace around the world; grant every nation the gift of living in perfect harmony with one another so together we can build a better world.

However, we know that there is evil all around us and many times this evil threatens our security and our freedom. In a just war, Lord, help me to defend my country with courage and promptitude. Free me from harming any innocent civilians. Protect me and my peers from any injury and from a sudden death. Teach me to be obedient to my superiors as long as their orders do not go against Your commandment. Keep my family safe and grant me the certainty that I will come back home safe so I may enjoy again the company and the love of my family.

Finally, allow me to always be aware that there is a greater war declared to us by our enemies: the world, the devil and the flesh. In this war, spiritual in nature, we all are soldiers fighting for our own salvation. Help me to keep my faith and fight the good fight (cf. 1 Tm 6:12) so that one day I may be able to enter into Your kingdom of glory and gazing upon the beauty of Your holy countenance to be counted among the hosts of Your angels and saints. Amen.

132. Prayer of a wife for the conversion of her husband

Lord Jesus, faithful husband of the Church, You are Good and Compassionate and Your mercy fills the whole world. In Your love, You called me to this beautiful vocation of holy Matrimony to which I wanted to respond with all my heart.

V Extra Prayers

Marriage, however, does not depend only on one person but on two. Unfortunately, the man I married does not know You nor does he live according to Your Gospel. Because of that he has been incapable of fulfilling some of the obligations to which we both committed ourselves at Your altar through our marriage vows. Forgive him, Lord, and forgive me for my own faults too.

Today I come before You begging for Your assistance and Your grace to have faith, patience, and wisdom to persevere in this difficult marriage. Grant me what I, in humility, ask You and change my husband's heart.

Your will, O Lord, is so great but sometimes difficult to scrutinize. It is not up to us to choose our crosses, but You in Your infinite wisdom give us the crosses we need for our own sanctification and the sanctification of those to whom we are united. Those crosses, however, never supersede the power of the graces You have placed within our reach.

Hence, trusting in Your mercy I beg You to look at my tears and at my heavy heart because of my husband's misdeeds. Gently come to his soul and give him the graces to know You and love You. Enlighten his mind and help him to faithfully observe Your commandments. Bestow upon him Your Holy Spirit so he can begin to live a deep and serious life of holiness. Send him the powerful company of St. Michael the Archangel to free him from the chains of sin, vice and the power of the devil under whose dominion he has decided to live.

You know, Lord, that I love with all my heart this man You have given me as husband *(if there are children the following is also said:* he is also the father of my children). It is because of this sincere love that I want what is best for his soul. Look with kindness on Your handmaid. I really want to help him to be holy as You, O Lord, are holy (cf. 1 Cor 7:14). Do not let death come to him without repentance and conversion.

Inspire in me what I should do to help him find You. Give me the firmness and the courage to stand up to him when necessary and also the tenderness and kindness to show him that it is not my intention to mortify him, but rather to be for him the companion of that true path of holiness that we started together on our day we exchanged our vows in holy Matrimony.

Listen, Lord, with kindness to my humble prayer accompanied by my many tears and my countless sufferings for the salvation of the soul of the man You gave me as a companion in this life. May we both praise You in this world and sing Your glories in Your kingdom for all eternity. Amen.

133. Prayer before dinner on Thanksgiving

O Lord of Goodness and Kindness, on this special day of thankfulness, we thank You for everything we are and for everything we have. We recognize that all of these come from You who loves us so much. Today, we give You thanks not only for this great food, lovingly prepared and beautifully presented, but also for so many special gifts You have given to this family and to all our friends that today - in Your Name -we welcome in this home.

Thank You for the comfortable place we live in, the beauty that surrounds us, for all the material goods, our health, spiritual wealth, our jobs, our enterprises and for everything we have. We also thank You for the struggles, for the crosses, for our illnesses and for all the problems we experience. We know, Good Lord, that through them You make us stronger and thus capable of helping to fill up in our own flesh what is still lacking in regard to Christ's afflictions (cf. Col 1:24). For this and for much more we thank You.

We know that the best way to give You thanks is by believing in Your Son Jesus Christ and by obeying Your commandments and so living according to the Gospel of truth that makes us really free. Do not allow any of us to depart from Your company but on the contrary, to grow each day in Your friendship.

Good Lord, we humbly ask You on this day to strengthen the union of this family, help us to care for one another, to forgive each other and to make this table a place where You may always be loved and praised. Bless our country, protect it from every evil and never allow it to depart from You from Whom all our rights come. May we always care for those who have less than we have. Once again thank You for Your love and for the gift of our faith in Your Son, Jesus Christ to Whom we are happy to welcome in the Eucharist and in the poor. Amen.

134.   Prayer to our Lady of Perpetual Help

O Mother of Perpetual Help, your beauty and holiness is superseded only by that of God, your Creator and Redeemer. Humbly and filled with confidence I invoke your powerful name, on behalf of the living and for the salvation of the dying, especially for those who today will leave this world.

Your beautiful image has miraculously accompanied the Church for most of her history becoming a perpetual sign for the Church of the East and the West that we share the same Mother who wants nothing else but our perfect unity in the true faith. Pray for us, O holy Mother of God.

    Purest Mary, let your name henceforth be ever on my lips. Help me to obey your inspirations and to be always attentive to your messages and commands. Teach me to see you always not only as my advocate and protector but also as a constant reminder that I have only so much time to turn my life completely toward your Son. Come, I beg you, always to my aid, Blessed Lady, to rescue me whenever I call on you. In my mortal life I struggle every day with different temptations which seek to snatch from me the salvation that your beloved Son, resting in your arms, gained for me. Do not allow the devil to use them to lose my soul forever.

    I give you thanks for the faith I have received and for the divine truths communicated to us by the Fruit of your womb, Jesus. My heart is filled with joy and happiness because without any merit on my part I have been found worthy of enshrining your name on my lips and calling on your assistance whenever I need your help. Therefore, I will never cease to call on you, ever repeating your sacred name.

    O Most powerful Mary be for me and for all those who have believed in your Son the perpetual help in our struggles so that crossing triumphantly by your hand this valley of tears we may one day contemplate the beauty of your Son's face.

Finally, O Mother of all graces, grant me the grace that every time I gaze upon the unique beauty of your image, I may grow in love for you and for your Son, my Lord and my God Jesus Christ. To Him I present my humble prayers trusting that from your holy hands, O Divine Mother of perpetual help, He will be pleased to receive them and generously attend to them. Amen. (*Say three Hail Marys*).

VI PRAYERS TO THE GLORIOUS SAINT JOSEPH

Etschied, Italy, July 14, 2018: Saint Joseph holding child Jesus, painting in the Saint Nicholas Church in Petschied near Luson, Italy

VI Prayers to the Glorious Saint Joseph

135.   Prayer to Saint Joseph on the mysteries of his life.

O great Saint Joseph, when you saw Mary for the first time, you loved her with such a love that for her you were willing to sacrifice everything you wanted in your life to help her fulfill the will of God and thus, cooperate in preparing the coming of the Savior of the world.

Help us to always put God's will first and find in it our happiness and our joy.

Hail Joseph, righteous man, the Lord is with you. Blessed are you among men and blessed is your faith and your obedience to God. Holy Joseph, Protector of the Son of God and His Mother, pray for us sinners, now and at the hour of our death. Amen.

Saint Joseph, faithful spouse of Mary, pray for us.

O great Saint Joseph, when the angel revealed to you in a dream that Mary was expecting a child from the Holy Spirit Whom God sent to save His people from their sins, without hesitation, you took Mary into your home and consecrated your life to raise and take care of the one who created the heavens and the earth (cf. Mt 1:20).

Help us to always be attentive to what God has to tell us and to faithfully carry it out.

> *Hail Joseph, righteous man, the Lord is with you. Blessed are you among men and blessed is your faith and your obedience to God. Holy Joseph, Protector of the Son of God and His Mother, pray for us sinners, now and at the hour of our death. Amen.*

Saint Joseph, obedient steward of God's household, pray for us.

O great Saint Joseph, when you arrived in Bethlehem and it was time for Mary to deliver the Divine Child, you found yourself in the situation of not having a place where Mary could give birth to her child. Immediately, you sought a suitable place until finally you found a humble barn, outside the city. There, with love and care, you transformed a simple manger where animals ate, into the place where heaven and earth met for the first time (cf. Lk 2: 1-12).

> Help us to never give up or despair when we find obstacles to doing what we are told by God and so always trust in His providence and assistance.

> *Hail Joseph, righteous man, the Lord is with you. Blessed are you among men and blessed is your faith and your obedience to God. Holy Joseph, Protector of the Son of God and His Mother, pray for us sinners, now and at the hour of our death. Amen.*

VI Prayers to the Glorious Saint Joseph

Saint Joseph, who trusted in God's providence, pray for us.

O great Saint Joseph, when the evil king searched for the King of Peace, who was under your protection, to put him to death, the angel came to you again in a dream, and told you to flee with Mary and her child into Egypt (cf. Mt 2:13). You, obedient and faithful, did as you were told and experienced the hardships of a life as an immigrant and stayed there until you received instructions from heaven to safely return home (cf. Mt 2:19).

>Help us to welcome and be kind to those who –because of persecution and violence- leave everything behind and come to our land.

>*Hail Joseph, righteous man, the Lord is with you. Blessed are you among men and blessed is your faith and your obedience to God. Holy Joseph, Protector of the Son of God and His Mother, pray for us sinners, now and at the hour of our death. Amen.*

Saint Joseph, immigrant of God, pray for us.

O great Saint Joseph, when the moment to leave this world came, God granted you a unique grace, that of breathing your last while holding the hands of the Light of the world, Jesus, and the Ark of the New Covenant, Mary, Most Holy.

Help us to always live our lives serving and honoring Jesus and Mary and so leave this world taken by their hands into a holy death.

Hail Joseph, righteous man, the Lord is with you. Blessed are you among men and blessed is your faith and your obedience to God. Holy Joseph, Protector of the Son of God and His Mother, pray for us sinners, now and at the hour of our death. Amen.

Saint Joseph, good and faithful servant, pray for us.

Let us pray

Father, You entrusted our Savior to the care of Saint Joseph. By the help of his prayers, may Your Church continue to serve her Lord and Founder, Jesus Christ, by always being faithful to His message and obedient to His will, through the same Jesus Christ, Your Son, our Lord, with You and the Holy Spirit forever and ever. Amen.

136. Prayer to Saint Joseph for the Church today

O powerful Saint Joseph, Protector and Custodian of the Church, you received from God Himself the mission to care, protect and look after His own Son and His Mother during those moments when they were most vulnerable. They were, indeed, with you included, the only

VI Prayers to the Glorious Saint Joseph

members of the Church that in those days and in their holy lives was beginning her existence.

Look with favor at the situation of this same Church in our days. Gaze upon her and see how she is being scorned, scourged, mistreated, and misrepresented by so many of those who were called to be her shepherds and her defenders.

Like Jesus and Mary, she is being persecuted in order to be silenced and eventually destroyed. Like Jesus and Mary, she suffers, but now in so many good bishops and priests who have understood like you did, that their mission is no other than to protect her and give their lives for her.

She also suffers in so many laity -little ones- who have believed in her faith and try to faithfully live it every day in the midst of a dark world, but many times without the support and encouragement of their own shepherds.

Do not allow, O great Father of love and gentleness, that the holy work of Jesus Christ, the holy Catholic Church, continue under the present state of confusion and darkness.

Come to her aid with the same courage with which you defended the Son of God and His Holy Mother from those who sought to destroy them. Disperse, and expel those children of this world who have infiltrated the Church in order to weaken and destroy her from within, and by that seek to eradicate from the world the message of salvation that Jesus brought, and that you and Mary were the first ones to so diligently listen and obey.

Come, O great warrior of God, who in silence fulfilled the will of the Almighty without any hesitation.

Bless and strengthen those bishops and priests who suffer persecution by their own fellow ministers because of their faith. Teach those men among the clergy and the laity to be real men and to assume the great responsibility to lead and govern the Church and their families, fearless of to what the world may say about them.

O Saint Joseph, great warrior of the Faith, the Universal Church acclaims you as her protector. Bring her peace and clarity as she implores from you your most efficacious, unfailing, and powerful guardianship against the forces of evil that try to slave her. Amen.

137. Prayer of a husband to Saint Joseph

Dear Saint Joseph, with profound humility I come to you to ask you to teach me how to be a good husband like you were to Our Lady, the Mother of God.

Help me to love my wife with that true love that never ends, that love that is filled with sacrifice and selflessness and that guided you to care for Jesus and Mary during the time you were with them in this world.

Guard my eyes and my thoughts so I may always be faithful to my wife and never fall into the temptation to look lustfully to another woman. Give me, hence, the grace of chastity.

Assist me with the necessary wisdom and knowledge to guide and raise my children as good Christians, that in their lives and in everything else they may always put God first.

Finally, o holy man who labored so hard to provide for your family by means of your honest work as carpenter, help me to always have work to provide for my own, and at the same time, do it with professionalism and excellence for the good of those I serve and for the glory of God. Amen.

138. Prayer to Saint Joseph during difficult times

To you, O blessed Joseph, do we come with confidence in the midst of our afflictions and struggles, in the midst of our sufferings and pains, and in the midst of our limitations and challenges, to beg you for your help and assistance. For the love you had and have for Jesus and Mary, we implore you to listen to our needs.

You better than anyone know how hard it is to work every day to put food on the family table during times of shortage.

- Give us the strength to work for our families and to meet their needs.

Hail Joseph, righteous man, the Lord is with you. Blessed are you among men and blessed is your faith and your obedience to God. Holy Joseph, Protector of the Son of God and His Mother, pray for us sinners, now and at the hour of our death. Amen.

O Saint Joseph, just man of God, pray for us.

You better than anyone know what is like to be hated and persecuted for fulfilling God's will.

- Give us the courage and the resilience to know that only God is necessary.

Hail Joseph, righteous man, the Lord is with you. Blessed are you among men and blessed is your faith and your obedience to God. Holy Joseph, Protector of the Son of God and His Mother, pray for us sinners, now and at the hour of our death. Amen.

O Saint Joseph, just man of God, pray for us.
You better than anyone, know what it is like to be an immigrant in a foreign land.

- Help those of us who live away from our land to be grateful to those who welcome us and to overcome all the difficulties that we may find in our way.
-

Hail Joseph, righteous man, the Lord is with you. Blessed are you among men and blessed is your faith and your obedience to God. Holy Joseph, Protector of the

VI Prayers to the Glorious Saint Joseph

Son of God and His Mother, pray for us sinners, now and at the hour of our death. Amen.

O Saint Joseph, just man of God, pray for us.

You better than anyone, know what it is like to give up your own plans for God's plans.

- Teach us to always obey God and conform to His will.

Hail Joseph, righteous man, the Lord is with you. Blessed are you among men and blessed is your faith and your obedience to God. Holy Joseph, Protector of the Son of God and His Mother, pray for us sinners, now and at the hour of our death. Amen.

O Saint Joseph, just man of God, pray for us.
You better than anyone, know what it is like to die leaving your family in the hands of God Himself.

- Give us the grace to always trust God, to work not for the food that spoils, but for the food that endures to eternal life (cf. Jn 6: 27). Help us likewise, when our time to leave this world comes, to find satisfaction in having accomplished our mission according to God's plan.

Hail Joseph, righteous man, the Lord is with you. Blessed are you among men and blessed is your faith and your obedience to God. Holy Joseph, Protector of the Son of God and His Mother, pray for us sinners, now and at the hour of our death. Amen.

O Saint Joseph, just man of God, pray for us

Let us pray

O most watchful guardian of the holy Family, defend those who have been redeemed by the Blood of Jesus Christ to Whom you looked after in this world. Gaze upon us, your servants, during these difficult times. Help us to grow in faith and to always know that the Good Lord will take care of us and of our families and will never abandon us. Give us, O great ally from heaven the grace of final perseverance in our way towards heaven where we will see you and enjoy the glory of Him you carried in your arms; that glory in which we know there will not be more suffering, nor pain and where we will want for nothing. Amen.

139. Prayer to Saint Joseph before leaving home

O most powerful Saint Joseph now that I momentarily leave my house, I humbly ask you to watch over my family, my children and those who remain in my home. Do it, O great Saint Joseph in the same way you watched and protected your home in Nazareth when in there dwelt the Word of God made flesh and His Mother, your dear Spouse, Mary Most Holy. Keep everyone safe, protect them from every evil and help me to return safely. As the head of this household, I have appointed you as our father and lord and as I do so I want to renew my faith and that of my family in the person of Jesus, your beloved Child, who we confess as our only Savior and Lord. Amen.

140. Ave Saint Joseph.

Hail Joseph, righteous man, the Lord is with you. Blessed are you among men and blessed is your faith and your obedience to God.

Holy Joseph, Protector of the Son of God and His Mother, pray for us sinners, now and at the hour of our death. Amen.

141. Prayer to Saint Joseph during a financial hardship

Dear Saint Joseph, most holy provider of the house of God, I find myself in financial difficulty for which I am unable to fully provide for my family. You, blessed Joseph, cared and provided for Mary and Jesus also during difficult times and it is for this reason that I come to you with great confidence.

O great man of God, help me to find soon the honest way to support and provide for my family during these difficult times.

I beg you, O greatest Knight of heaven, graciously listen to my plea which I direct to you today. So many saints have come to you in similar situations and none went away disappointed. I have the assurance that I will not either. I ask you this in the name of Jesus and through the intercession of Mary most holy who wanted for nothing while under your loving and solicitous care. Amen.

142. Prayer to Saint Joseph asking for a holy death

O Glorious Saint Joseph, triumphant patron of a holy death, who, before you had the blessing to close his eyes to this world gazing at the beauty and radiance of the countenances of the Son of God and His Mother? Nobody. That makes you the happiest man to leave this world before the work of redemption carried out by our Lord Jesus Christ.

Today I humbly beg you, when God calls me from this world into His presence, give me the grace to have the time to be prepared, and do not allow me to die from a sudden and unexpected death. Help me to leave this world in peace and holiness, having had the time to repent and be freed from my sins, to receive the graces of the sacraments and finally, to have you and Mary by my side. Then, while closing my eyes to this world gazing upon your unfathomable and beautiful faces, I will rejoice at the assurance that Jesus will be merciful to me when I stand to be judged before His Throne of Justice and Truth. Amen.

143. Family consecration through Saint Joseph

All: In the name of the Father and of the Son and of the Holy Spirit. Amen.

Father: Dear Saint Joseph with love and humility I come to you with my entire family in this act of consecration. The Lord of heavens and earth entrusted you with the life of His Son and His Mother at the beginning of the time of redemption, and you fulfilled that mandate with unseen love and courage. To me, also, the Good Lord has entrusted with the care of this family, my family which I love very much. Thus, as the head of this household, I want to invoke your name and your protection.

All: *Dear Saint Joseph to you we consecrate our family*
Mother: O great man of God, hear the prayers of this family that today rejoice for the privilege of welcoming you into this house. Teach us, first and foremost, to love and serve God and also to serve and love one another. Help my husband and me to make our home a place of love and kindness, especially for those in need. Teach us to make our home a place where God may always be loved and adored and never insulted or offended by us, our children or any of our guests.

All: *Dear Saint Joseph to you we consecrate our family*
Father: Teach me how to love my wife and to treat her not as a dictator or a tyrant but as you treated Mary, that

is, with kindness and respect as a companion in our common path toward holiness.

Mother: To me also, good father, grant me the grace to be like Mary your Holy Spouse and to be for my husband a help and support so he can find in me the same help that you found in Our Lady.

Father and Mother: Help us together to be good to our children, to raise them according to God's law and according to the true faith, and to understand them and guide them through their struggles as they grow and mature into young men and women.

All: *Dear Saint Joseph to you we consecrate our family*

Children: To us, dear Saint Joseph, help us to give our parents the same obedience and respect that Jesus gave to you and Mary even though as God and Lord, he had the whole creation subjected to Him. Make us grow in grace and stature like Jesus did under your protection and by your example. Bless our parents, and do not allow Dad (or-and Mom) to ever lose his (her or their) job (s) and help us to behave so that they may be proud of us.

All: *Dear Saint Joseph to you we consecrate our family*

All: Help us all to be a faithful image of the family that you formed with Mary and Jesus. That in our home and in our lives we may be govern and guided by the principles of the Gospel and not of the world. Free us from any kind of hatred, envy, fighting for power or domination, arrogance, wrath, retaliation, resentment or any other

VI Prayers to the Glorious Saint Joseph

sentiment that destroys this unity that, through God's grace, we enjoy today.

Father: Dear Saint Joseph this is your home, and you are always welcome here. Bless my family and help me to provide for them, not only materially but above all spiritually.

All: *Dear Saint Joseph to you we consecrate our family*

Mother: You, Saint Joseph, are called the Terror of Demons, free us from all evil, protect us and our children from the influence of a world of death and darkness and help us to work not for the food that spoils, but for the food that endures to eternal life (cf. Jn 6: 27).

All: *Dear Saint Joseph to you we consecrate our family*

All: That by your intercession we may live in this life in obedience to God and that after this life, we may be worthy to receive the grace to see each other in heaven together with Jesus and Mary in the glory of God that never ends. Amen

(End the consecration with three Hail Joseph)
Hail Joseph, righteous man, the Lord is with you. Blessed are you among men and blessed is your faith and your obedience to God. Holy Joseph, Protector of the Son of God and His Mother, pray for us sinners, now and at the hour of our death. Amen.

All: In the name of the Father and of the Son and of the Holy Spirit. Amen.

Prayers of the Soul

144. Liliary to Saint Joseph

We call the Rosary the prayer in which we honor Mary because it is a gift of many roses (prayers). One gives roses to Mary because she is a woman, but to Joseph we do not give roses but lilies, which is the sign of his purity, so I think we should call this prayer emulating the Rosary, Liliary to Joseph.

In the name of the Father and of the Son and of the Holy Spirit. Amen.

The Apostles' Creed

I believe in God, the Father almighty,
creator of heaven and earth.
I believe in Jesus Christ, his only Son, Our Lord.
He was conceived by the power of the Holy Spirit
and born of the Virgin Mary.
He suffered under Pontius Pilate,
was crucified, died, and was buried.
He descended to the dead.
On the third day he rose again.
He ascended into heaven,
and is seated at the right hand of the Father.
He will come again to judge the living and the dead.

I believe in the Holy Spirit,
the holy catholic Church,
the communion of saints,
the forgiveness of sins,
the resurrection of the body,
and the life everlasting. Amen.

VI Prayers to the Glorious Saint Joseph

One Our Father and Three Hail Maries

First Mystery:
Joseph receives the message of the Angel in a dream.

"Because Joseph her husband was a righteous man and was unwilling to disgrace her publicly, he resolved to divorce her quietly. But after he had considered this, an angel of the Lord appeared to him in a dream and said, 'Joseph, son of David, do not be afraid to take Mary home as your wife, because what is conceived in her is from the Holy Spirit. She will give birth to a Son, and you are to give Him the name Jesus, because He will save His people from their sins'" (Mt 1: 19-21).

Grace: Almighty God, through the intercession of Saint Joseph give us the grace of always thinking the best of others, never condemning anyone and being attentive to your voice.

One Our Father and ten Hail Joseph.
Hail Joseph, righteous man, the Lord is with you. Blessed are you among men and blessed is your faith and your obedience to God. Holy Joseph, Protector of the Son of God, and His Mother, pray for us sinners, now and at the hour of our death. Amen.

Glory be to the Father …

O my Jesus forgive us our sins save us from the fires of hell, lead all souls to heaven especially those in most need of your mercy.

Joseph, most blessed servant of God, grant us the grace to die as you did, gazing upon the faces of Jesus and Mary.

Second Mystery:
Joseph takes Mary with child to Bethlehem.

"In those days Caesar Augustus issued a decree that a census should be taken of the entire Roman world. (This was the first census that took place while Quirinius was governor of Syria.) And everyone went to their own town to register. So, Joseph also went up from the town of Nazareth in Galilee to Judea, to Bethlehem the town of David, because he belonged to the house and line of David. He went there to register with Mary, who was pledged to be married to him and was expecting a child" (Lk 2: 2-6).

Grace: Almighty God, through the intercession of Saint Joseph give us the grace of discernment so we can put into practice in the best possible way your will in our lives.

One Our Father and ten Hail Joseph.

Hail Joseph, righteous man, the Lord is with you. Blessed are you among men and blessed is your faith and your obedience to God. Holy Joseph, Protector of the Son of God, and His Mother, pray for us sinners, now and at the hour of our death. Amen.

Glory be to the Father …

O my Jesus forgive us our sins save us from the fires of hell, lead all souls to heaven especially those in most need of your mercy.

VI Prayers to the Glorious Saint Joseph

Joseph, most blessed servant of God, grant us the grace to die as you did, gazing upon the faces of Jesus and Mary.

Third Mystery:
Joseph flees with Jesus and Mary to Egypt

"When the Magi had gone, an angel of the Lord appeared to Joseph in a dream. 'Get up! he said. 'Take the Child and His mother and flee to Egypt. Stay there until I tell you, for Herod is going to search for the Child to kill Him'. So he got up, took the Child and His mother by night, and withdrew to Egypt, where he stayed until the death of Herod. This fulfilled what the Lord had spoken through the prophet: 'Out of Egypt I called My Son.'" (Mt 2: 3-15).

Grace: Almighty God, through the intercession of Saint Joseph give us the grace of courage and fortitude especially during times of difficulties and darkness.
One Our Father and ten Hail Joseph.

Hail Joseph, righteous man, the Lord is with you. Blessed are you among men and blessed is your faith and your obedience to God. Holy Joseph, Protector of the Son of God and His Mother, pray for us sinners, now and at the hour of our death. Amen.

Glory be to the Father …
O my Jesus forgive us our sins save us from the fires of hell, lead all souls to heaven especially those in most need of Your mercy.

Joseph, most blessed servant of God, grant us the grace to die as you did, gazing upon the faces of Jesus and Mary.

Prayers of the Soul

Fourth Mystery:
Joseph established himself with Jesus and Mary in Nazareth.

"But when he heard that Archelaus was reigning in Judea in place of his father Herod, he was afraid to go there. Having been warned in a dream, he withdrew to the district of Galilee, and he went and lived in a town called Nazareth. So was fulfilled what was said through the prophets, that he would be called a Nazarene" (Mt 2: 22 23).

Grace: Almighty God, through the intercession of Saint Joseph give us the grace of seeking holiness in living the lives You have called us to live, no matter how small or unimportant they may seem to be.

One Our Father and ten Hail Joseph.

Hail Joseph, righteous man, the Lord is with you. Blessed are you among men and blessed is your faith and your obedience to God. Holy Joseph, Protector of the Son of God and His Mother, pray for us sinners, now and at the hour of our death. Amen.

Glory be to the Father …
O my Jesus forgive us our sins save us from the fires of hell, lead all souls to heaven especially those in most need of Your mercy.

Joseph, most blessed servant of God, grant us the grace to die as you did gazing upon the faces of Jesus and Mary.

VI Prayers to the Glorious Saint Joseph

Fifth Mystery:
Joseph dies next to Jesus and Mary.

Sacred Scripture does not tell us how Joseph ended his life, but the apocryphal literature does. According to it, he died of old age accompanied by Mary and Jesus. If this episode were mentioned in the Bible, it will probably say something like this: *"After a very holy and long life at the service of God through Jesus and Mary, Joseph, son of Jacob, died in Nazareth holding the hand of Mary, his wife, and Jesus to Whom he raised as his own son."*

Grace: Almighty God, through the intercession of Saint Joseph give us the grace of a holy death.

One Our Father and ten Hail Joseph.

Hail Joseph, righteous man, the Lord is with you. Blessed are you among men and blessed is your faith and your obedience to God. Holy Joseph, Protector of the Son of God, and His Mother, pray for us sinners, now and at the hour of our death. Amen.

Glory be to the Father …

O my Jesus forgive us our sins save us from the fires of hell, lead all souls to heaven especially those in most need of Your mercy.

Joseph, most blessed servant of God, grant us the grace to die as you did, gazing upon the faces of Jesus and Mary.

145. Litanies to Saint Joseph

Lord, have mercy on us.	**Lord, have mercy on us.**
Christ, have mercy on us.	**Christ, have mercy on us.**
Lord, have mercy on us.	**Lord, have mercy on us.**
Christ, hear us.	**Christ, graciously hear us.**
God the Father of heaven,	**have mercy on us.**
God the Son, Redeemer of the world,	**have mercy on us.**
God the Holy Spirit,	**have mercy on us.**
Holy Trinity, one God,	**have mercy on us.**

Mary, Mother of God	**pray for us**
Saint Joseph, Faithful Spouse of Mary	**pray for us**
Saint Joseph, earthly father of Jesus	**pray for us**
Holy and chaste man of God	**pray for us**
Holy man filled with grace	**pray for us**
Holy man of humble heart	**pray for us**
Holy man of great power	**pray for us**
Holy man of unsurpassed integrity	**pray for us**
Holy man of unwavering faith	**pray for us**
Holy man of unbreakable hope	**pray for us**
Holy man of supernatural love	**pray for us**
Holy man of perfect obedience	**pray for us**
Just and righteous herald of God	**pray for us**
Kind and Pious Father	**pray for us**
Man most pure	**pray for us**
Man most venerable	**pray for us**
Man of great courage	**pray for us**
Man of justice	**pray for us**
Knight of Glory	**pray for us**
Lover and servant of the cross	**pray for us**
Temple of obedient silence	**pray for us**

VI Prayers to the Glorious Saint Joseph

Prudent and valiant gentleman	**pray for us**
Master of redemptory suffering	**pray for us**
Trusted by God Himself	**pray for us**
Steward of Heaven	**pray for us**
Tower of Protection	**pray for us**
Provident and infallible ally	**pray for us**
Friend and father of all the saints	**pray for us**
Mont Sinai of the New Covenant	**pray for us**
First Warrior of the Kingdom	**pray for us**
Model of workers	**pray for us**
Pillar of families	**pray for us**
White Martyr of the faith	**pray for us**
Guardian of the Divine Logos	**pray for us**
Teacher of the Eternal Wisdom	**pray for us**
Master of the Word	**pray for us**
Instructor of the Truth	**pray for us**
Guide of the Way	**pray for us**
Vessel of devotion and piety	**pray for us**
Vessel of pure and holy love	**pray for us**
Universal Patron of the Church	**pray for us**
Solace of the afflicted	**pray for us**
Terror of demons	**pray for us**
Impeccable Mirror of the Gospel	**pray for us**
Fortress of interior life	**pray for us**
Impenetrable fortress of faithfulness	**pray for us**
Holy Envy of the prophets	**pray for us**
Joy of the Patriarchs	**pray for us.**
Admiration and Owe of the Angels	**pray for us**
Blessed at the hour of death	**pray for us**
Good and Faithful servant of the Lord	**pray for us**
Father and lord of the Church	

   R. Come to our aid
Help us to grow in the true faith

R. And bless us with good, holy and faithful bishops and priests

Do not allow our beloved Holy Catholic Faith to be corrupted

R. And protect us from bad and cowardly shepherds

In the battles and struggles of our lives

R. Be our protection and our companion

When doubt and fear knock at our door

R. Teach us how to expel them from our hearts

Blessed Saint Joseph patron of Holy death

R. Grant us the grace to die in your company, in Jesus' and Mary's.

Final Prayer

O great Saint Joseph we have remembered and meditated on the mysteries of salvation in which you gave us a great example of love and faithfulness to God, intercede for us, do not allow us to fall into temptation, protect and save the Church and help us to walk this world as you did, obedient and loyal to God in serving our families as you did with yours. Amen.